Trading
with the
Enemy

Trading
with the
Enemy

SEDUCTION AND BETRAYAL ON JIM CRAMER'S WALL STREET

Nicholas W. Maier

HarperBusiness
A Division of HarperCollins*Publishers*

HarperCollins books may be purchased for educational, business, or sales promotional use. For information please write: Special Markets Department, HarperCollins Publishers, Inc., 10 East 53rd Street, New York, NY 10022.

FIRST EDITION

Production by Stratford Publishing Services, Brattleboro, Vermont

Library of Congress Cataloging-in-Publication Data
Maier, Nicholas W., 1968–
    Trading with the enemy : seduction and betrayal on Wall Street / Nicholas W. Maier.
        p. cm.
    ISBN 0-06-008651-3
    1. Wall Street.   2. Hedging (Finance).   3. Speculation.   4. Cramer, Jim.   5. Stock brokers.   I. Title.
    HG4572 .M25 2002
    332.64'5—dc21   2001039929

02 03 04 05 06 QBF 10 9 8 7 6 5 4 3 2

FOR
BETH
AND
CORINNE

Acknowledgments

Mom, Dad, and Drea—for being there from the *very* start.

Jessica and Brad—for believing in my writing, even before they should have.

Mark Kantor—for Wednesday Shirt Day.

Marc H. Glick and Stephen F. Breimer—for being agents, editors, lawyers, and friends.

Joe Veltre, Sarah Beam, and Deborah Klenotic—for helping to make this book all that it could be.

Lisa Berkowitz—for supplying her marketing genius.

Shari and Eric—for thinking of me while stuck on a plane.

And especially Matthew Guma—for giving life to this book. Without him, *Trading with the Enemy* would not be.

Contents

Contents

Trading
with the
Enemy

Prologue

WINTER CAME EARLY in Cambridge, Massachusetts, that year. Having graduated college six months before, I was living at home with little direction or desire, convinced my destiny would be to grow old and gray at my parents' dinner table. It's strange how memories can be colored—certain springs remembered as more brilliant, other autumns as particularly dull—all because of some kind of success or struggle. I recall that time, late 1993, only as an especially cold and dark period. The snow piled up on the sidewalks and temperatures dipped well below normal.

One evening, I bundled myself into a thick coat and ventured out of our house, a small white colonial. Pulling my collar up and a wool hat down over my ears, I made my way along the quiet, icy street, past a few doors to the home of the Peretzes. Their house was equally modest, despite an expansive backyard that covered close to an acre. I had spent many summer nights running from end to end of this neighborhood oasis with my childhood friend, Jesse, his younger sister Bo, and their family dog, Bandit, a husky with one blue eye and one brown.

I kicked the snow from my shoes while ringing the bell. My friend's father, Marty, wanted to see me.

Martin Peretz was prominent in political and cultural circles for his liberal politics at the helm of the magazine he owned and edited, *The New Republic,* but he had always been simply Marty to me. My childhood was filled with pleasant activities that included the Peretz family, each as vivid as Bandit's different-colored eyes: playing with Jesse and Bo under a weeping willow across the street from their home; having Marty take us to see movies at the Fresh Pond Cinema in their old brown Jeep Cherokee; and being welcomed every year by Marty and his wife, Anne, to a Passover Seder, thoroughly dull to a kid except for the incredible desserts and the hope of a $20 reward for finding the hidden matzoh.

The close friendship between Marty and my father dated back to their days as graduate students at Harvard. Their bond was more of an intellectual one than that between Jesse, Bo, and me, which was based on listening to the Beatles, playing catch, and watching television. Unable to leave their college days behind, our fathers sought and secured permanent residences at Harvard. Marty lectured on political theory, and my father became a professor of European history.

In the foyer, Marty gave me his usual warm, tight hug, and led me to the living room. We sat down and chatted about the miserable winter weather. It wasn't long before he steered the conversation toward my goals, going so far as to ask if I had any "career aspirations." I wondered for a moment if sleeping late and still making a lot of money fit into this category.

To say that I saw Marty as *only* Jesse's dad and a neighbor would not be entirely truthful. By this time I had recognized that he wasn't your typical neighbor. I met famous writers, musicians, politicians, and all kinds of prominent people at Marty's Seders. Although from the outside his home appeared modest, the interior was anything but. Renoir, Picasso, and Corot originals hung on the light beige walls. Expensive tiles from Israel covered the floors of the rooms, which were separated by wood doors from the Middle Ages. After all, not just *any*body puts you on hold to answer a call from Al Gore. I understood that Marty "knew people."

More than anything else, I felt respect for Marty. I recognized him to be sincere in his kindness, an individual who had earned my father's friendship through years of loyalty. My father once told me that "if anything ever happened" to him and my mother, Marty was the person my two sisters and I should go to. I saw this as the ultimate sign of approval.

I told Marty about my mostly eclectic and unfocused interests. I was thinking of law school, as so many literature majors with little ambition beyond making a living are apt to do. My work experiences were rather limited. I had painted a lot of houses, both inside and out. I could drive a shuttle van proficiently. That fall I had tried scalloping in Nantucket Bay, although after nearly drowning in two feet of water, I crossed fishing off the list. Somewhere between indecision and outright confusion I managed to tell Marty about a recently acquired obsession—the stock market.

I had been stashing every dollar I earned from my various pursuits in a low-interest-rate savings account, but after a brief lecture from Grandpa Rubbelke, that came to an end. Grandpa explained that at my age, he had bought three hundred shares of Saint Jude Medical. What then cost him a few hundred dollars was now worth over a million. Not only that, he raked in $10,000 a year just in dividends.

I transferred my money to Fidelity the next day. I was soon spending all my free time reading up on technology and transportation, health care and hospitality companies. Opening the paper to read the tables or listening to Dan Dorfman on CNBC, the top-rated business news channel, I saw nothing but opportunity. My small bookcase quickly filled with investment magazines. I was going to follow in my grandfather's footsteps and make a fortune *fast*.

This revelation interested Marty. As fate would have it, a friend of his had found enormous success playing the market. His name was James Cramer.

Jim was a Harvard Law School student when the two first met. Despite his commitment to law, Jim was being pulled in another direction. An avid follower of stocks, he left hot tips on his answering machine. After one of these recommendations proved successful, Marty put a decent chunk of his money in Jim's care. That money quickly grew and was eventually placed with a limited partnership known as Cramer & Company, a hedge fund run by Jim and his wife, Karen, with more than a hundred million dollars under its management. That winter, Cramer & Company was closing a seventh year of outperforming the Standard & Poor 500 and the Dow.

In telling me of Jim's meteoric rise, Marty painted a picture of someone not unlike myself. Jim was intelligent and wanted to make money. He believed law might be the way to go, but the prospect of reading briefs for days on end didn't do it for him. Trading stocks did. Our stories were quite similar, except that Jim went on to make millions, whereas I was living with my parents. I liked his ending better.

Jim often wrote articles on the market that Marty published in *The New Republic*. Marty said he could speak to Jim on my behalf and see if he might be able to arrange for a position to be offered. I could indulge my new interest under the guidance of "one of the best in the business."

Quickly growing excited at the prospect, I envisioned myself as a VIP with a special pass to the world of Wall Street. I was ready to pack up my room, tell my girlfriend, Beth, she could find me in New York, and hop on the train. Surely this was the chance of a lifetime.

I had no compunctions about taking an opportunity born solely of connections, having met enough accomplished people to recognize that success was not always predicated on talent alone. Life was just as much who you knew as what you knew. After all, Jim Cramer had obviously benefited immensely from knowing Marty.

I spent the next five years, 1994 through 1998, at Cramer & Company. What I learned about the business was from my experience there; what I learned about Jim came straight from the horse's mouth. During my time at Cramer & Company, there must have been hundreds of articles written about the man, but I read only a few. I got enough of him twelve hours a day, five days a week.

The question that sticks with me to this day is why I stayed as long as I did. In retrospect, I believe that my initial resolve and overwhelming desire to do whatever it took to succeed kept me hanging on when I should have let go. It was not until the bitter end of 1998, after dedicating everything I had to Cramer & Company, that I finally found myself walking out the doors, never to return.

Chapter 1

"TWENTY-TWO-FIVE AND ALL THE HANOVER DELI FOOD YOU CAN EAT"

"HE'S BUSY," the Cramer & Company secretary said to me when I tried to contact Jim. "Call back after the close."

"Call back after you're closed?" I asked, confused.

"After *the* close."

"*The* close? The close of *what?*"

"The *market!*" she screamed and hung up.

After a little research and a few more hours, I tried again. At 4:15, the secretary told me to "try again tomorrow." The next day was the same thing all over again. A week later, I finally got through.

"I can waste a few minutes now," were Jim's first words to me.

I had memorized a long speech, complete with my 110 percent commitment to Cramer & Company, about why Jim should hire me. Before I could even open my mouth, Jim told me not to bother. There was no room for me. This discussion was taking place only as a favor to Marty. Someone without market experience would be a "hindrance" to his operation, he said.

After this ten-second exchange, I hung up the phone and realized that what sounded too good to be true had been just that. I felt more desperate than before my meeting with Marty. Once I had mentally put myself in New York City, working for Jim Cramer's hedge fund, my previous career ideas seemed impossibly unexciting. Granted, I still didn't know who Jim Cramer really was, or what exactly a hedge fund did, but I had made up my mind that it was all pretty good. I went back to Marty, and the "misunderstanding," as he put it, was quickly worked out; a meeting with Jim arranged.

My interview at Cramer & Company in January 1994 was the first time I had ever gone to New York City on my own. I arrived at Penn Station on an Amtrak train, stuck my wallet in my sock, and prepared to die. All I knew of the city were the things I read every day in the *New York Times* metro section. The day before I arrived, a baby had been tossed out with the garbage, someone had been pushed in front of a subway train, and a taxi driver had purposely run over a bunch of pedestrians. The thing about New York is that at first you're scared you might get murdered, but after staying a few days you're more worried about killing someone else.

A light snow fell from the dark sky as I approached the front of 56 Beaver Street. On the ground floor of the eight-story brownstone was a closed restaurant, Delmonico's, which must have been quite a scene at one time, judging from the elegant mahogany tables and crystal chandeliers that collected dust inside the windows. The building sat at the juncture of five small streets in the heart of Wall Street, and was fitted like a slice of pie into the angle formed by Beaver and Stone Streets, with the front door of the restaurant facing the intersection. Skyscrapers loomed above, permanently shading the corner. Wearing a cheap gray suit my father had bought me the day before, I pressed the Cramer & Company buzzer. It was 6:30 A.M.

Jim Cramer met me at the front door of his seventh-floor office, shook my hand, and sized me up with beady brown eyes. Kinky dark hair jutted out in hectic spikes around the sides of his balding skull. About five foot nine and husky, maybe two hundred pounds, he stood sweating and breathing heavily, his jaw clenched. I wondered if he'd been running around in the office before I rang.

"I get in every morning *very early*," Jim announced.

He turned and quickly led me down a narrow hallway laid with worn green carpeting, past cheaply framed *New Republic* covers emblazoned with his name.

"I was just on a conference call talking with Lou Gerstner, the CEO of IBM," he said, sticking a finger under his collar and trying to loosen his tie. Although barely conscious at the time, I realized Jim had probably done more that morning than I would do all week.

We entered headquarters for his operation: a small, triangular room almost completely filled by a long, U-shaped gray Formica desk. The desk consisted of six connected workspaces, each piled with three or four monitors, and lots of oversized phone turrets that all had two receivers and more than fifty lights. Wires ran everywhere.

"This is the trading room," Jim said. He directed me to an empty seat while taking his own at the head of the desk. His chair was at the vertex of the room, directly above the restaurant's front door. Behind him was one of two filthy windows in the room that couldn't be opened or, apparently, washed. The walls looked like they hadn't been painted in years. Here and there magazine articles were posted up with thumbtacks. Upon closer inspection, I saw they were all about Jim.

"I sit here from the moment I get in until I leave at night," Jim explained, fiddling with a computer mouse to remove the screen saver on his center monitor—a picture of himself smiling that resembled a publicity shot. Preoccupied with paperwork, newspapers, and the market data in front of him, he only occasionally glanced in my direction.

"I'm on the trading desk *all* day."

"Updating your systems?" I asked, noticing unopened boxes of new computer parts piled up against a wall behind Jim's chair.

"What?" He turned a page of the *Financial Times*.

"New monitors . . ." I pointed.

"Oh, those . . ."

"Jim, this is obviously an awkward situation for both of us." Feeling uncomfortable and more like an imposition than anything else, I decided I had nothing to lose by being candid. "I understand you don't want to give me a job just because Marty wants you to, and, truthfully, neither do I."

This seemed to get Jim's attention, and I saw my opportunity. I went on, "I'm truly fascinated by what you do, and if you have the time, I'd just like to hear your story."

It was as if night turned to day. Jim looked right at me and broke into a wide smile. He started with the story of how he and Marty had met, giving me the specifics on the millions of dollars he subsequently made for Marty. He told me about his days as a Goldman Sachs broker before he started the hedge fund with his wife, Karen. He gave me the details on how earlier that morning he had "helped Lou out" on their conference call. I was amazed to hear him refer to such a prominent business leader by his first name. I pictured a Rolodex stuffed with the phone numbers of high-powered friends.

"*This* is my life," Jim said, throwing his hands up in the air and looking around the tight confines. "*All* I think about is the stock market, the stock market, and then I think about the stock market."

"It obviously hasn't been a waste of your time," I said. "You've been a huge success."

"I'm a *player* now," Jim conceded.

This was the first time I heard Jim use the term, but it wouldn't be the last. A player was someone who knew how things worked, commanded a lot of money, and could move the market. A player was someone to listen to. Everyone wanted to be one, but few really were. Simply put, a player was a Wall Street insider. I immediately understood that to be a player was *very* important to Jim.

"Twenty-two-five," Jim said as he walked me back to the elevator later that morning. "Twenty-two-five and all the Hanover Deli food you can eat."

"Sounds like a good deal to me," I answered without a moment's hesitation, simultaneously overjoyed at being called into the game and terrified at not knowing how it might turn out. At least I would get to the plate.

It was still a good two hours before the market opened, but the sun had come up and the sky was clear. Turning against the tide of workers flooding from the Lexington Avenue Express stop, I walked past the J.P. Morgan building and the New York Stock Exchange, approaching Trinity Church. Here I was, on Wall Street, soaking in the sights like any other tourist. Except I wasn't a tourist—I belonged.

Chapter 2

"RICHER THAN GOD"

"TWENTY-TWO-FIVE is a lot more than I made when I started out in the world," Jim said as I stepped onto the elevator to leave that morning. I had been there close to an hour all told, listening nearly the entire time to him carry on enthusiastically about his many great achievements. As the doors closed between us, he grinned from ear to ear and added, "Now, I'm richer than God."

I figured Jim meant he was a millionaire. After all, I still hadn't figured out how in the world I would spend *twenty-two thousand dollars* in *only* a year.

It wasn't long after I arrived on Wall Street when it hit me that I had been absurdly conservative about Jim's wealth.

To appreciate the potential rewards of running a hedge fund, you need to understand what a hedge fund does. A hedge fund is merely an investment firm. Its goal, as with any investment firm, is to make money. What differentiates a hedge fund is its approach to the business.

Take the usual mutual fund. You can send your money to Fidelity, Janus, Alliance, or any of the thousands of mutual funds that fill the last few pages of every newspaper's business section. There's usually a pretty low minimum investment, anywhere from a few hundred to a few thousand dollars. You can pick a sector, such as technology or health care, or a style, such as value or growth. Exactly what a fund intends to do with your assets is usually laid out in its annual prospectus.

Most mutual funds keep to relatively strict charters. Many of them, for instance, are not allowed to sell short. To "sell short" is to sell shares of a stock that you don't own in the first place. Your broker lends you shares that are being held in another account. The idea is to return the shares later at a lower price so you can pocket the difference. Picture it exactly like a regular buy and sell, but reversed. You sell a stock high first, and then buy it low to close out the position. Basically, selling short is a way to profit from a declining stock.

Besides restrictions against selling short, mutual funds are governed by other rules and regulations intended to limit the risk posed to the public investor. Many do not use leverage, which is to borrow against existing capital to make a bet that is larger than actual assets. Some are restricted from having any single position that amounts to more than a few percent of their overall portfolio.

Mutual funds are supposed to operate within the guidelines of what most people consider responsible investing.

The typical mutual fund is designed to go "long," the opposite of short. Going "long" is just another way of saying what most of us do, which is make bets that the stocks we selected will increase in price. The fund buys shares in what it believes to be good companies and, for the most part, attempts to ignore the intermediate vagaries of the overall market. Mutual fund managers are therefore essentially paid to pick stocks, not to be market timers.

At a hedge fund, on the other hand, almost anything goes. A hedge fund is so named for one of its original purposes, to be "hedged," or to go both ways. The idea was to structure a fund so it could be long and short simultaneously. Some call this a "market-neutral" strategy. The original hedge funds were intended to perform in any economic environment. A manager was able, even expected, to capitalize on both the ups and the downs of the market.

What these funds evolved into, however, is not at all what they were originally named for. There is now nothing hedged or neutral about most hedge funds. Rather than focusing on balancing its long and short exposure, the modern-day hedge fund takes advantage of its liberal charter to do all sorts of transactions. The newest players make huge bets on countries or currencies, sectors, or individual stocks. They might be net short, 500 percent long, or anything in between. Volatility is the only sure thing with most hedge funds.

Hedge funds are created as a "limited partnership," which makes them a private entity, unlike their public mutual fund brethren. Restricted to include only "knowledgeable" investors, the "general partner" is allowed to engage in strategies that might not be suitable for "normal" individuals. In plain English, this means that the Securities and Exchange Commission wants only rich people to let someone like Jim Cramer play with their money. The aggressive trading of hedge funds poses risks too great for mom and pop to bet their life savings on. More important, their private structure allows hedge funds to avoid much of the scrutiny that mutual funds attract from the SEC.

In the stock market, with risk there ideally comes reward, and this certainly holds true for both the investor in a hedge fund and its manager. Relying on the very strategies that mutual funds are prohibited from using, hedge funds have been known to outperform their conservative relatives. If it hadn't been for the success of pioneers like George Soros, hedge funds might never have proliferated. Such trailblazers made fortunes for the people willing to wager on them and paved the way for the thousands who have followed in their footsteps.

Of course, out of all the people Soros made rich, the person he made the richest was himself.

Most mutual funds typically take only a small management fee. There is little direct reward for good performance, except for the effect it might have on assets under management. Experience a bad year followed by investor withdrawals, and you have fewer assets to take your management fee from. Have a good year, develop a track record, and the assets add up. If a mutual fund gets to be the size of Fidelity's Magellan, $100 billion, three quarters of 1 percent is a lot of money.

Hedge funds, on the other hand, usually take 1 percent a year for expenses and 20 percent of the profits. A few hedge funds have taken up to 50 percent, but Cramer & Company stuck to the more traditional share. Essentially, hedge funds say to their wealthy investors, "If you make money, we make money." Consider what is gained in a good year. Take a $100 million hedge fund and factor in a 20 percent return. The fund makes $20 million. The manager takes 20 percent of that, and suddenly on top of the $1 million management fee, a $4 million performance bonus is gained. It doesn't take a genius to do the math and realize how lucrative this business can be.

In the 1990s, as one of the strongest bull markets in history ran straight through the roof, the number of hedge funds grew exponentially. Consider a $100 million fund, small by industry standards, and factor in an 80 percent year, as the Nasdaq Composite returned in 1999. A manager might personally make more than $16 million. Many hedge funds, including Cramer & Company, had *far* more than $100 million and experienced spectacular returns during this period. Not a bad paycheck, even after bonuses go round to analysts, traders, and Uncle Sam.

So now you want to start a hedge fund? The hardest thing is finding investors. You need a lot of rich people, or a few *really* rich people, to trust you with their money. Remember, this is a limited partnership, typically allowing only a hundred people to participate. If you take a thousand bucks from every relative you can think of, the fund will have a whopping $100,000. Even with a 100 percent return, after collecting a management fee and performance bonus you'll make only $21,000. In Manhattan, that doesn't even pay for parking.

You need to find individuals who are willing to invest at least a few hundred thousand. People in the industry usually use $10 million as the minimum starting point of capital. This means you should have at least that much from all partners put together. Not that you couldn't start with less, but that's the level often used as a benchmark. With $10 million, in a 20 percent year, you'll collect half a million bucks. Now you can park your BMW *and* buy gas. Start trading, and after a year or two of decent returns, assets will inevitably grow.

Jim found his initial investor, Marty, to be a great start. Marty, like most wealthy people, knew other wealthy people, and he referred these friends to Jim. Jim had also worked for a few years as a broker at Goldman Sachs Private Client Services, a division for only the richest of the rich. Unless you have $10 million, don't call Goldman PCS. Even if you have fifty, don't expect a quick call back.

Between Marty, Marty's friends, and the few clients with whom Jim had already demonstrated his abilities, Cramer & Company was started. When I arrived in 1994, Jim was managing around $150 million. The fund peaked at around $400 million going into 1998. Most of those years, Jim brought home seven- to eight-figure bonuses. Much of that money went back exactly where it came from—into the fund. Add into each performance bonus what Jim made on his existing nest egg, and the money became astounding, even by today's inflated standards.

So you can add a few zeros onto my initial estimate of what Jim meant that first day.

Maybe he *was* richer than God.

Chapter 3

IN THE FOXHOLE

A FEW HOURS AFTER getting the job, I was following an apartment broker around to the "cheaper" areas of Manhattan (all of which have subsequently disappeared). By the time we walked into our first studio, I had already agreed to pay twice what I'd expected. When I saw the studio, I realized it was for half of what I'd hoped.

The place was on East Houston, a two-way cross street wider than a highway, and certainly louder. My broker pitched this location as "convenient to everything." About the smell of urine in the lobby she announced triumphantly, "The landlord intends to clean that up!" The oversized cockroach lying on its back in the middle of the single dark room was proof that the "exterminator has done his job!"

"What a plus!" I replied.

If you find a decent apartment in Manhattan, you have about two minutes to come up with the money to secure it. I thought the broker was lying about this until we finally came across an apartment that wasn't on a highway, didn't have piss in the lobby, and showed no sign of cockroaches. Before I could get a pen to my checkbook, it was gone. Somebody quicker had scooped it up. After I bought my broker lunch, which was a requirement, we were off and looking once again. A few days later I finally had the privilege of paying the woman a fee of 15 percent of one year's rent.

My cubbyhole was at the corner of Thirty-ninth Street and Lexington Avenue in Murray Hill. It was on the ground floor, so I quickly found myself on display. Every time I opened the blinds passersby stared in at me. They critiqued my few items of furniture, my posters, and my tiny, messy kitchen. I soon understood exactly what it felt like to be a caged animal in the zoo.

The noise was also relentless. The first time Beth called, she wondered why I was taking calls at a pay phone.

"This is my own phone!" I screamed as fire trucks wailed down the street. Besides the typical car alarms, there seemed to be a nightly barrage of jackhammering outside my single window.

Just when I thought it couldn't get any worse, I came home one afternoon to discover another unexpected charm to my neighborhood. As I walked down Lexington from Forty-second Street, the sidewalks, even the streets, were jammed with people. Crowds screamed and yelled and held up signs. It took me half an hour to push my way through the mob just to get to my front door. I was living right next to the Cuban mission. Not only that, but the half of Cuba that had come to America was outside my apartment. There was a demonstration nearly once a week, usually on Sunday afternoon right around nap time.

One morning, after another restful evening pleasantly filled with the buzz of a chainsaw, I climbed off my futon at 5:30. It was time to start earning my twenty-two-five. I put on my one and only suit and walked the few blocks to Grand Central Station to take the subway downtown for my first day of work. Out of the mouth of a narrow stairway from the street down to the trains poured an endless stream of people, and I stood off to the side, wondering if I was at an exit. Finally, I followed the lead of a brave individual who walked dead on into the coming tide.

Buying a token, I asked the person in the booth if she had a schedule. She told me the schedule was for me to go down to the platform and sooner or later the train would come. She was right.

At 6:30, Jim opened the front door to the company offices with a pained expression on his face. "Let yourself in, next time." He turned and rushed back down the hallway to his seat on the trading desk. Flying by the secretary, he said, "Deal with him."

While Jim returned to his screens, I was introduced one by one to the people I would be working with.

"I suppose you could come into my office," said Jeff Berkowitz, Jim's director of research, as he led me toward the back. Jeff was a young guy, about six feet tall with short brown hair, and he wore ratty jeans with a black polo shirt tucked in. I already knew that he was Jim's right-hand man. Marty and Jim had each alluded to this fact, describing him as a "hot shot" and a "whiz kid."

"Mine is the *only* private office," he announced, kicking his Gucci loafers up on the desk in front of him. "Even Jim doesn't have his own office . . . So, what were your SAT scores and GPA?"

Before I could answer, Jeff launched into a detailed personal history. He had been an associate analyst at Goldman Sachs under a technology analyst named Dan Benton. Jim hired Jeff as he was completing his MBA at Columbia University. His first bonus, after working a summer for Jim, was $30,000. He was going out that night with a beautiful blonde who had very expensive tastes, which was definitely *not* a problem for him, he said.

I was supposed to be impressed by all this, and, to be honest, I was. The first time I met Jeff, I saw someone I wanted to be. He was four inches taller and, as he made clear, infinitely richer and more successful. Whereas I entered Cramer & Company as little more than an intern, Jeff was already on top of the world.

What Jeff had that I really wanted, however, wasn't the material things (not that I would have complained), but rather his responsibilities. This guy, barely older than me, was entrusted to play an integral role in the day-to-day decisions regarding the investment of millions of dollars. The fact that both Marty and Jim expressed such confidence in Jeff was what I most admired.

After Jeff dismissed me, the secretary took me around the desk, introducing me to the traders. The head trader was Mark Kantor, a short, forty-something guy with thick glasses. He wore plaid golf pants that Rodney Dangerfield would have envied and a loud green shirt.

From the start, Mark was friendly and genuine. He asked me a few questions about myself and seemed interested in the answers. He was also the only one in the office who made jokes, and he always laughed at his own punch line. After finding me a chair, he invited me to watch what he was doing. He explained a few of the basics, like the difference between a bid and an offer and how to read a quote line. Then, after placing a trade, Mark showed me the transaction going by on the consolidated ticker tape.

"Everybody in the world just saw our trade!" he shouted. I felt the excitement the exercise was intended to provoke. "Just like being on TV!"

"I wouldn't know," I replied.

"You will some day. But for now, this will have to do!" Mark cracked up laughing.

"I'm busy now," said Sal Schillace, the options trader, when I was sent in his direction. With much effort, he extended a hand, and I shook his sweaty palm. Then Sal returned to surfing the Internet. He had dark hair parted down the middle of his forehead and clothes that looked as if they came straight out of the Sears catalogue. Sal's desk was decorated with sports team memorabilia, which reminded me of my own room at home when I had been ten.

"Rangers fan, eh?" was all I could come up with to say.

"That's fucking obvious."

"Okay," I replied as the secretary, in an act of compassion, pulled me away.

Finally, I met Clark Longwell, whom Jeff and Jim had referred to as a "clerk." He had a serious, quiet demeanor, and hair with touches of premature gray that made him look older than he actually was. From Texas, Clark spoke with a heavy southern drawl.

"My name isn't really Clark," he said in a voice barely above a whisper so only I could hear.

"No?"

"No. My real name is Larry. But everyone here calls me Clark. You should just call me Clark."

"Okay, Clark. Why?"

"The Cramers told me I could have this job, but I couldn't be Larry. They had a previous business partner named Larry. It ended *badly*."

One cannot speak of Cramer & Company without mentioning Jim's wife, Karen Cramer, whom Jim called the "Trading Goddess." Karen had been a trader at a hedge fund run by Michael Steinhardt before she met Jim.

I perceived Karen as a very calm person. I suppose I never would have noticed this quality about her if it hadn't been in such sharp contrast to her husband. Where Jim was frenetic and wild, Karen seemed calculating and coolheaded. They must have made a good trading pair, like counterweights keeping a scale even. I sensed immediately not to mistake her apparent subdued nature as a sign of weakness. Like Jim, she had an intense glare that warned, "Don't waste my time with useless pleasantries."

"So, Jim tells us you're a seasoned investor," Karen immediately commented in front of everyone. "Is that right?"

"A regular Warren Buffett," I joked. No one in the room except Mark laughed.

"So, Warren," Karen moved on, "do you consider yourself a long- or short-term investor?"

"Do I consider myself a long- or short-term investor?" I repeated, stalling. Despite my grandfather's influence getting me here, I found I lacked his patience. My desire to make money *yesterday* led me to trade in and out of nearly everything I bought.

"I usually only hold onto things for a few months," I finally answered. "That would make me a short-term investor."

Everyone on the desk cracked up.

This most definitely made me a long-term investor, Karen corrected, as she stood up to leave. She was eight months pregnant with their second child, Emma. It was her departure that had opened up a spot for me.

Sitting there that day, I looked around at the people to whom I had just been introduced. Three feet to my left was Clark. Next to him was Mark, no more than another arm's length away. To my right sat Jeff. Next to him was Sal. Completing the small circle was Jim, directly across from me.

These five people would soon become a greater part of my life than even my girlfriend or immediate family. I was to spend more time in direct contact with them than I had ever spent with anyone. There would be almost no private conversations for the next five years. The idea of personal space was a thing of the past. We would all eat breakfast, lunch, and often dinner in this cramped room.

As I looked across the desk to see Jim glued to his monitors, just as he had been that first time we met, I realized that if I leaned down ever so slightly, I sunk below his line of sight. I could *almost* hide. Little did I know how often I would end up doing exactly that.

A few hours later, shortly after the opening bell, Jim got upset over a trade that went wrong. He was trying to buy five thousand shares of Intel and gave Mark the order. Mark picked up the phone and passed the order on to a broker exactly as Jim told it to him. A minute later, the broker called back to give Mark the report, and Mark repeated the confirmation to Jim.

"You bought five thousand Intel at a quarter," Mark said. In certain situations, as I would soon learn, it was appropriate to leave off the "handle," or the round-number part of a price, to save time.

"That's wrong," Jim replied.

Mark picked up the phone and asked the broker again for the price.

"A quarter," Mark repeated.

"I said that's wrong," Jim said as his lips tightened and his eyes narrowed. "The stock was offered at an eighth when you called."

"Well . . ." Mark seemed unsure how to handle the situation. I looked around the desk to see Sal making the same face as Jim.

Clark had his head down and was punching an average into his calculator. Jeff got up and went into his office.

"Well, what?" Jim snapped, and suddenly stood. "I told you it was offered at an eighth when we called!"

Jim was convinced he should have bought the stock for 12½ cents cheaper. The difference was $625.

"That broker just fucked us, big time!"

"The eighth offering was fading when we called," Mark explained. "Fading" meant that any stock that could have been bought at an eighth was going fast when Jim gave the order. That was why Jim wanted to buy in the first place. He saw people taking the stock. Mark maintained that the broker was justified in giving us a quarter report.

Jim bit down on his lower lip as his hands clenched into fists. He leaned forward to get closer to Mark, and started banging on the top of his monitors. The crown of his balding skull reddened as he yelled at the top of his lungs in a high-pitched whine.

"I told you they *fucked* us! *Fucked* us, *fucked* us, *fucked* us!"

His hands flew up to the sides of his head and started pulling at his few wisps of hair. He kicked a metal garbage can across the room, sending trash all over the floor. It landed with a thud against the wall, a big dent in its side. No one else said a thing.

"*Listen to me.*" With piercing eyes Jim scanned our sober faces. "This is not some *fucking* joke!" he screamed, spit flying from his mouth. "We are at war. We are in a foxhole." He flung out his hands. "*Everyone* out *there* is the *enemy!*"

Mark nodded to show Jim that he understood. That wasn't what Jim wanted. He started smashing his phone over and over on the desk in front of him. He lifted a monitor and heaved it like a shot put. After flying several feet, it shattered on the floor.

"We are at war. We are in a foxhole. *Everyone* out *there* is the enemy!"

Chapter 4

"ANSWER THE FUCKING TRADING LINES!!"

AFTER MY HARSH INTRODUCTION to New York City, I quickly became accustomed to all kinds of things. The constant Cuban protests outside my apartment were now a chance to practice my Spanish. I charged headfirst down the stairs at Grand Central, leading the way for others as I had once been led. Even the sounds of the jackhammers, car alarms, and fire trucks all blended together like the crashing of waves.

I also recognized very early that there was one rule to be adhered to above all others at Cramer & Company. Every morning after I walked through the front door of our trading room and took my seat at the desk, I was expected to disappear. No one spoke until Jim spoke. No one ordered lunch until Jim ordered lunch. No one left until Jim left. Not one of us was supposed to do a *thing* without his cue. Soon enough, I followed the example, and learned when to do what. We each had a limited role, and that was as far as it went. This was Jim Cramer's show, and we were all merely props on his stage.

Despite my attempts to acclimate myself, there was one thing I would never be able to ignore. From that first day on, I woke up every morning just after 5:00, a good half hour before my alarm went off. Saturdays, Sundays, holidays—it didn't matter. At a few minutes after 5:00 my eyes would open, and I was seized with a sense of panic and uncertainty. My forehead was always damp with sweat, despite the fact that my blankets lay on the floor next to the bed, having been kicked off during a night of constant tossing and turning. The only thought on my mind was *get to Cramer & Company.*

Jim always went into the office at 5:30 A.M., or so I heard. Jeff followed him in around 6:00. The rest of us were expected shortly after that. I walked through the door each morning and encountered the same face that had met me on day one. Jim's clenched jaw and direct stare announced to all of us that our situation had not miraculously improved overnight. We were still at war.

It wasn't long before I realized how swift the shelling could come and that most of it, in fact, might be friendly fire.

A few days after I began, I was given my first job: answering the phone. I figured I could handle it. How hard could answering a phone be?

I was sitting at the trading desk, listening to Jeff tell me about the date he had the previous evening, when the outside line rang.

"Answer the fucking phone," Jeff instructed, pointing to the turret.

I lifted the receiver. "Cramer & Company."

The caller casually asked to talk with Jim.

"I'm a friend," he explained. "Jimmy's expecting my call."

With some instruction from Jeff, I managed to forward the call to Jim's private line, and watched as he picked up the phone and said hello. A second later the phone was back in its cradle.

"If you send through another salesman, swear to god . . ." Jim bit his lip while shaking his head. A pencil was stabbed into the notebook before him.

"If you send through another salesman, swear to god . . ." repeated Sal. Mark just laughed as Clark crouched over and whispered to me not to *ever* put another salesman through to Jim.

"You can't let just *anyone* talk to Jim!" said Jeff. "Ask them who they are and what the call is regarding," he added before starting on about his BMW. I learned it was a black four-door 528 before the outside line rang again.

"Cramer & Company," I answered. Once again someone asked for Jim. I had no intention of making the same mistake twice, especially since everyone on the trading desk was now watching me. I asked the person who he was and what the call was regarding. After giving his name, the man insisted he was a friend.

"Sure," I said. "I know. You're his *best* friend, just like the *last* guy who called." I put the man on hold, and after a while he finally hung up.

"Who was that?" Jeff asked.

"Another salesman. Eliot Spitter, or something," I laughed. Everyone just looked at me, mouths hanging open, so I added, "Spitter, now *that's* a stupid name!"

"That was Eliot *Spitzer*, you fucking moron!" Jim screamed. Eliot was, in fact, a friend of Jim's. One Jim would later throw a fundraising party for when he pursued the New York State attorney general's office, which he eventually won. We invited every broker who covered us to that party, kept track of who came, and, most important, noted who contributed to Eliot's campaign. The smart brokers made sizable donations and were rewarded for it. The others didn't place too many trades for Cramer & Company over the next few months. I, for one, gave $50 and never again forgot his name.

"There are certain people you have to just put through to Jim," said Jeff, wagging an index finger.

"But you just told me—"

"I *know* what I told you, and *now* I'm telling you to figure it out. If you can't answer a stupid fucking phone right . . ."

"That was Eliot *Spitzer*, you fucking moron!" Sal reiterated. Mark was obviously finding something amusing while Clark crouched over and whispered to me not to *ever* put Eliot Spitzer on hold again.

As the room sat in dead silence, the outside line rang again. I tried to ignore it, hoping it would stop ringing. It didn't. Everyone looked at the red light blinking on the phone. I was thinking that someone else might pick it up. No one did.

"Are you going to *answer it?*" Jim asked through gritted teeth.

"Cramer & Company," I said after picking up the receiver, wishing that this call would be for someone, *anyone*, besides Jim.

"Is Jim there?"

"Who's calling, please?"

"Max."

"What's this regarding?"

Everybody on the desk bent forward, cringing with the expectation that I was screwing something up yet again. They were right.

"Is Jim *there* or *not?*" Max asked impatiently.

"What's the call regarding?" I tried to find out for a second time.

"Tell him it's *MAX!!!*"

All I could think to do was put him on hold, and I turned to ask Jeff if he knew who this Max was.

"Someone you just should have put through to Jim!" Jeff retorted.

Max happened to be an important partner. I learned this as Jeff retreated to his office, recognizing that I wasn't the best person to be associated with at that time. I soon learned that whenever things took a turn for the worse, Jeff demonstrated an uncanny ability to be gone *before* the shit hit the fan.

"Jesus fucking Christ," Jim said, staring at me as if I had leprosy and shaking his head disapprovingly once again before lunging for the phone. "What the fuck is wrong with you?"

"Jesus fucking Christ, what the fuck is wrong with you?" parroted Sal. Mark only laughed while Clark crouched over and whispered to me that I should *always* put partners through to Jim right away.

The partners, as I would learn, were *the* most important calls. They were the few extremely wealthy individuals whose assets comprised the $150 million that Jim played with every day. I was to memorize each of their names and treat them as royalty. Like Marty Peretz, who called every morning, most partners checked in on a regular basis.

Jim bent over backward for the partners. He would step out of meetings, interrupt any personal conversation, and put them ahead of *anything* else. He could be trading like a madman and screaming at the top of his lungs, but when a partner called he dropped whatever he was doing. His entire demeanor flipped from Mr. Hyde to Dr. Jekyll. As soon as he picked up the phone, he was civil and eloquent, saying things that we otherwise never heard come out of his mouth, like "please" and "thank you."

Each day the action soon escalated to a feverish pace. There were a few outside lines on the phones, which I answered, but most were direct links to our various brokers. The turret lit up like a Christmas tree, and Jim, Mark, Sal, and Clark couldn't handle the volume.

"Answer the trading lines!" Jim screamed, looking helplessly around the desk.

Although I still didn't have a clue what any of the traders or Jim was actually doing, I figured I'd follow their example. Everyone else was standing, so I decided to stand up, also. That was obviously what you did when trading became intense. Except I wasn't doing anything, while they all jumped from light to light frantically and screamed at one another. Finally, as they all juggled two phones at once and the trading lines still *kept ringing*, Jim leaned over his terminals and looked straight at me.

"Don't just sit there like a fucking idiot!" he screamed. "I said *answer the fucking trading lines!*"

Without thinking of the consequences, I hit the light that said "Morgan Stanley" and someone yelled something at me really fast—all I caught was "sold ten shares at fifty." From what I saw the other guys do, I figured I was supposed to tell Jim whatever the caller told me. Jim had a phone to each ear and was saying something into one while listening to the other. I yelled to him that he sold ten shares at fifty.

Everyone just looked at me *again* and I wasn't sure why, so I repeated myself.

"Sold 'em at fifty! All ten shares!"

Jim slammed both his phones down on the desk and shrieked, "*Mother fucking ten shares!*" His voice was a high-pitched whine and he sounded like he just might explode.

"You!" Jim leaned over the desk to get within a foot of Mark's face. "Teach him how to answer the *fucking trading lines!*"

"Ten shares? *Ten shares?*" Sal added. "Ten shares costs like . . . like . . . a hundred bucks, for Christ's sake! We've *never* traded only *ten* shares!" Sal was making the exact same face as Jim, looking as if he had swallowed a lemon.

Mark walked over to me. "That was ten *thousand* shares of Merck we sold with Morgan Stanley at *fifty-one and a half,*" he calmly explained. "At least you got the fifty part right." He placed a pencil in my hand, threw some scrap paper next to my monitor, and told me to write these details down while the brokers were on the wire.

"You're the customer," Mark said. "You can ask them to repeat themselves."

So it went the first few days. I continued to put the wrong people through to Jim and the important ones on hold. When answering the trading lines, I mixed up share quantity with price and reversed buys and sells. The scrap paper didn't come in handy until I figured out later how to write as fast as the brokers talked. For each blunder, I was cut to shreds by Jim and then, of course, by Sal.

It wasn't long before my hit ratio improved. Whereas initially I screwed everything up, I was soon getting a *few* things right. Mark continued to try and teach me from my mistakes. Clark whispered instructional warnings as Sal jumped down my throat. The third day I was there, without thinking twice, I picked up the Goldman Sachs line . . .

"Goldman has five hundred thousand IBM going on the tape at the figure, open buy!" I relayed with little understanding of what it meant, but managing to get each detail correct.

"I buy fifty thousand shares on that print!" Jim shot up out of his seat and screamed with both arms pointing toward me. "I buy fifty! *Buy buy buy buy buy buy buy!*"

"I buy fifty thousand shares on that print!" Without missing a beat, I repeated the order to the broker. "I buy fifty! *Buy buy buy buy buy buy buy!*"

A moment later we were done.

"Bought your fifty thousand shares of IBM at the figure," I told Jim.

Clark jotted down the report on the blotter in front of him. Jim returned to his seat, and Sal started picking up the other lights now blinking on the turret. I saw Mark smiling over the monitors at me, and I couldn't help but crack a grin. I had just made my first trade.

Soon enough I was standing with them all, screaming as if I'd been doing it my entire life. This was pretty much what it would be like all day every day on the Cramer & Company trading desk. It was controlled chaos, some days less controlled than others. Things could and would get insanely busy at any minute. We'd all be placing orders, taking reports, and juggling five things at once. In the midst of all this, by February of that first year, I learned to trade both equities and options.

I understood everything from the basics of placing an order to the more complex strategies that Jim was implementing. There were "buy-rites," "married puts," "synthetic shorts," "spreads," and "collars." These all were complicated option and stock strategies that Jim implemented every day. I took the sheets home at night and studied the positions. I calculated where they became profitable and how Jim could structure the portfolio to benefit from volatility—upward or downward.

I had always been the type who learned by doing. At Cramer & Company, no book smarts would have helped, anyway. It was trial by fire. I was cut down and miserable when I screwed up and thrilled when I managed to get something right. The thing about the stock market I liked the most was that when we applied our strategies, the market graded us immediately. There was no test at the end of the week. Money was made or lost instantly. In no time at all, I was a junkie for the action, just like Jim.

Chapter 5

A *VERY* IMPORTANT QUESTION

EVERY MORNING a little after 8:00, a barrage of calls came in from the brokers. Major houses like Goldman Sachs, Bear Stearns, and Morgan Stanley made comments each day, including upgrades and downgrades on specific stocks. Notebook in hand, Jeff emerged from his office to confer with Jim at the head of the trading desk on how this information might affect the marketplace. Since Jim *never* left his monitors if at all avoidable, this was where most of the brainstorming had to be done.

One morning after I'd been at the firm a few months, Jeff stepped from his huddle with Jim and called me into his office. I was going to start doing "research," he informed me. This would require a sharp mind and a deep intellect, he went on. I needed to understand the strategy that came before the trade was placed.

"In this business," Jeff explained, "one always has to use one's head."

Before I might actually begin to do something dangerous like think on my own, Jim wanted to talk to me. He called me over to his station at the head of the trading desk and, speaking in a low, serious voice, gave me the specifics of my first assignment.

"Your mission," Jim said, "is to ask a *very* important question."

"Got it," I replied.

"Why don't you wait until I tell you *what the fuck* to do," Jim said through a locked jaw.

"Okay," I agreed.

Jim began to explain point by point, leaving as little room for error as possible.

"There is a company called Hannaford Brothers, which is a supermarket chain. At 1:30 this afternoon, they are making a presentation in midtown at a Lehman Brothers conference. I want you to go to this presentation. You will put your hand up, and ask them, 'When are you going to have to lower your earnings numbers because of all those stupid fucking acquisitions you made?' After you ask this question in front of everyone, I want you to follow Hannaford into the 'breakout session,' and then ask the same question again. Got it?"

"Got it!" I replied. Then, also in a whisper, I went so far as to ask, "Why?"

"Just ask the fucking question!" Jim barked, glowering up at me from the monitors to convey that I had severely overstayed my welcome.

I pulled a suit from the closet where we kept more formal attire for just such occasions, and went into the bathroom to change. Before I headed uptown, Jeff called me back into his office. He started telling me about the *two dates* with *two different women* he had planned for the coming weekend.

"Wow," I said and looked *very* impressed.

After giving me more details than I wanted to know about the restaurants they would be going to, China Grill and Gotham, and the limousine they were taking, a stretch, he added that it might be better if I worded Jim's question a little differently.

"Oh, by the way," Jeff added. "Don't bother signing up. You're only going to be there for an hour or so."

"Signing up?" I asked.

"Just don't get a nametag, all right?"

This was the first conference I'd ever even been to, and after searching for half an hour to find the right room, I went into a meeting with close to five hundred analysts. While the CEO of Hannaford Brothers narrated slides of frozen food aisles, I frantically tried to memorize my question, which Jeff had written down for me. I figured I would look better if I could ask it without reading it off a scrap of paper.

Finally, when the lights went on, I got up and shot my arm to the air. I was sweating and shaking, but I knew I *had* to do this.

Other people had their hands up, but I was the only one standing. The CEO called on me.

"Due to your recent acquisitions of new stores," I asked as loudly as I possibly could, "isn't it likely that you might have to reconsider certain overly optimistic profit assumptions?"

The CEO stalled for a minute, an annoyed look on his face, before responding, "Sorry, I can't answer that."

I looked around the room to see a few people looking as dissatisfied as me with this reply.

I sat down. "Sounds like this joker has something to hide," I whispered to the person next to me.

The breakout session was a much smaller meeting, with only about twenty people. I followed the CEO into this, determined to get to the issue at hand. Hannaford Brothers had made some acquisitions, and I wanted to know what the effect would be on their bottom line. The bottom line, as Jeff had explained, is the net earnings line on an income statement. Now that I knew what it actually meant, I was all the more eager to get to it.

"Maybe *now* you can answer the question?" I asked.

"I *told* you I *can't* answer that! We're in our *quiet* period," he said, clearly vexed.

"Shhhhhh," I whispered to my neighbor, bringing a finger to my lips. "They're in their *quiet period*." I wondered if this was something that occurred right before nap time.

"An eighth? An *eighth?*" Jim was pacing back and forth behind his monitors yelling at Mark when I got back to the office. "Oh, *please!*

Just take me out and *rape* me by the woodshed, why don't you! I could pay a guinea pig to execute orders better!"

"I'm not sure if that's true," Mark argued.

"*Oh, it's true!*" Jim snapped, nodding his head up and down, arms crossed in front of him.

Before I had long to wonder how badly I had screwed up this one, Jim looked at me and commented, "I guess you asked the question." By this point, I had learned to measure everything Jim said on a relative basis. Considering all the other things he was screaming, I took this as a glowing compliment.

I sat down at the trading desk and punched up HRD, the symbol for Hannaford Brothers, to see that the stock was down close to a point. Clark leaned over and whispered to me that we shorted fifty thousand shares of it that morning and had just "covered it," or bought it back, profitably.

Later that afternoon, along with learning about Jeff's pending summer share in the Hamptons, I discovered what a quiet period actually is. In the few weeks before a company reports earnings, they are restricted by the SEC from commenting on anything related to those earnings. Jim must have known that the CEO would have to decline to answer the question, and he was apparently hoping that just the assertion they had something to hide might spook someone. I don't know if Jim's question was why HRD dropped, but he obviously thought it worth a try. Apparently, a large seller materialized around the time I was heckling the guy.

On the train home that evening, I began to put together a few variables. Some of the method behind the company's madness was becoming clear. Jim essentially used me to ask a loaded question. The reason Jeff didn't want me to sign up wasn't just that I would be in and out so quickly. He didn't want me to be wearing a Cramer & Company nametag. To ask Jim why he wanted me to pose the question had been asking for *far* more than I needed to know. But I was starting to figure it all out on my own.

I had absolutely no problem with any this. I knew that Jim made money year in year out at this game. What I didn't yet know was how. I wanted only to be a sponge, soaking up the wisdom of my mentor. No matter what the situation or level of artillery he fired, Jim would look around the room and announce the same thing:

"This is Wall Street. This is what we do."

If this was the way Jim fought, then this was what I wanted to learn.

Jim continued to send me out to presentations and lunches, sometimes with softball questions intended to make a given company look good or bad, sometimes simply to listen. I also still worked on the trading desk and flipped millions of dollars' worth of equities every few minutes. Now I was taking the morning research calls from all the various brokers, relaying upgrades and downgrades as they occurred. On the rare occasion when there was time, I traveled up and down the Street to get a view of how things were done at other firms.

At the NYSE I was given a tour far more intimate than the crowds behind the glass would ever see. I followed a floor broker around to all the various specialists' posts. I screamed "buy!" and "sell!" in frantic crowds. I gazed up from the center of it all at the cavernous ceiling of the Garage, throwing scraps of paper into the air that fluttered down onto the littered ground.

I watched the opening of the market at the Goldman Sachs Nasdaq desk. I witnessed hundreds of people crammed into a gym-sized room all start to shout when the clock hit 9:30. Intel, Cisco, and Microsoft trades of twenty, fifty, a hundred thousand shares raced across the oversize ticker tape on the far wall. For an entire hour I was privy to orders coming in from Fidelity, Alliance, and Wellington, and you could bet *these* players moved the market.

I sat at Lehman Brothers with market makers and watched them try to buy and sell almost as frantically as Jim. They explained the "spread" they tried to always earn. They cursed the clients just as Jim cursed the brokers. I recognized there was a mutual animosity that ran up and down the Street, all of which revolved around the same ingredient—money. I suppose this should not have seemed like a great insight.

Yes, at Cramer & Company I had to answer the phone, and I was regularly at the vendor's cart at the corner of Wall and Water, picking up twenty soft pretzels with plenty of mustard. I knew Hanover Deli's phone number by heart. But after ordering four black coffees and two fruit cups, I bought twenty thousand shares of IBM and listened to a conference call.

I've met a lot of people who have gone through more traditional training programs at the major brokerage houses. Starting out at Goldman Sachs or Merrill Lynch, you might learn how to trade equities or bonds or do sales or analysis. You might even spend a few months doing each, but you would never do them all at once. At Cramer & Company, I was tossed headfirst into the entire game.

Before I knew it, weeks turned into months. The environment didn't get any easier. It was stressful and nasty. The anxiety I awoke to every morning did not subside. But the near terror of not knowing what awaited me behind the door at 56 Beaver Street in the morning almost always gave way to a deep satisfaction when I walked back out in the evening. I was learning and doing more than I ever could have hoped. I was dealing with Wall Street from the front row. The place itself could be crazier than Bellevue, but I was far too busy to notice.

Chapter 6

"CHE-CHING!"

JIM CRAMER LOVED to tell people how it was done. Barely a week went by without his appearing on television, being quoted in some major publication, or writing a financial article. If a reporter from the *New York Times* called, Jim could rattle off the particulars of nearly any company on the fly. If he was writing a feature for *The New Republic,* he could spew a thousand words of complex market theory in minutes flat. Dressed in his high-priced Zegna suits and Thomas Pink ties, Jim would go on the *Charlie Rose Show* and exhibit an understanding of the global economy as good as any and better than most.

"I speak to *hundreds* of public companies a week," Jim told a prospective partner over the phone one of the first days I was on the trading desk. "I'm doing research *all* the time. In this business, you have to stay on top of *every*thing. I was *just* on a conference call, talking with Lou Gerstner, the CEO of IBM."

All portfolio managers would have you believe they get their ideas from old-fashioned digging. The right way to make money, by most standards, is through hard work and experienced insight. Just as a well-known commercial intoned, a fund must "earn" its returns. By most standards, investing has nothing to do with trading. There is a socially acceptable investment model, and in public Jim Cramer constantly reaffirmed that he understood this.

Having been a reporter before pursuing more lucrative interests, Jim certainly valued extensive research. He spent countless hours flipping through the brokerage house publications that flooded our office. He also read trade magazines like *American Banker, PC Magazine,* and even *Supermarket News.* He started each day flipping through close to twenty newspapers from around the country. My hands were often black from pulling the business sections out of the *Boston Globe, San Francisco Examiner, Chicago Tribune, Houston Chronicle,* and *Miami Herald.*

Jim and Jeff routinely spoke with companies and other analysts, seeking out industry trends or company-specific news. They listened to conference calls and dissected earnings. Margins were scrutinized and tax rates determined. Complicated, esoteric things like "DSOs" and "LIFO credits" were uncovered. The two constantly reassessed the terrain.

In private, however, Jim Cramer played a far different game. Although our firm was more than capable of conducting its business in the manner of a traditional investment fund, to say that we always operated this way would be lying. Any type of patient, considered strategy was routinely forsaken for another approach. The primary idea at Cramer & Company was to make "fast money"— lightning quick analysis and nonstop trading.

Jim's true trading philosophy was encapsulated in a note he had stuck to the center monitor at his workspace:

"It's better to be lucky than good."

These words of wisdom contributed to more investment decisions than meticulous research did at Cramer & Company.

A prime example was when Jim flew to California to visit Max Palevsky, one of the fund's wealthiest investors. Max was a billionaire industrialist who invented the logic chip, but, more important, he lived in Los Angeles and had many famous friends. During this visit, Jim got the chance to hang out with a few movie stars.

As soon as Jim was back in the office, he started telling us all about his Hollywood encounters. Apparently he had met Candace Bergen, Max's neighbor, who somewhere along the way ordered "one of those Starbucks drinks, a Grande-Latte-Mocha-Cappuccino-Icy-Thingamajig," as Jim called it.

"Candy loves those things! They are *unbelievable* and well worth the five bucks," Jim went on. "Mark, buy fifty thousand shares of Starbucks. I'm telling you, Candy knows what the fuck she's talking about when it comes to these things!"

The Candace Bergen indicator proved prescient, as that evening Starbucks reported their latest sales figures, far exceeding Wall Street estimates. We sold the shares the next day for a quick $100,000 hit.

Then there were the "Swimming Tunes." Karen, who had been enjoying her time out of the office doing laps at the pool, discovered this great new device at an Authentic Fitness store. It was a small waterproof radio and headphones. As any experienced trader does, she spotted the trend.

"Who *wouldn't* listen to the radio while swimming, now?" Jim asked the following morning.

"No one wouldn't!" we all agreed.

"Mark, buy me fifty thousand shares," Jim ordered. He beckoned me over to him. "Go and check this thing out," he whispered, nodding his head up and down as if to say, "I think we know what you'll find."

By the time I was on the subway heading uptown to the closest Authentic Fitness store, we had our position on the sheets. Sure enough, there were no Swimming Tunes to be found at the store, and the clerk told me they were sold out. At the second store, I managed to scoop up the last pair.

Back at the office, I produced the goods and everyone gathered round.

"That does look pretty cool," Jeff acknowledged.

"I'll say," added Mark.

"Great idea, Jim," said Sal.

"They were sold out at the first store," I chimed in.

Clark nodded with approval.

It couldn't have been more than a few hours later that ASM declared they would be buying back a million shares of their own stock, and we flipped our fifty for a quick point. Later, when their investor relations representative finally called me back, she told me to return my radio for a refund. No, they weren't sold out, as the clerk at the first store told me. They had been pulled from the shelves because of complaints of electrical shocks.

Occasionally, outright mistakes yielded better results than thoughtful investments. Once Jim was out of the office, a rare event, and called in to Sal to have him buy five hundred CBS calls.

"Buy five hundred?" Sal asked.

"Buy five hundred!" We all heard Jim's voice through the phone as if he had been in the next room.

Five hundred option contracts were the equivalent of fifty thousand shares of common stock. This was no small order.

When Jim came into the office later that afternoon, the calls Sal bought had increased a good 20 percent.

"Hey Jim, whatever tip you got, it was a good one!" Sal said the moment Jim walked in.

"What the *fuck* are you talking about?" Jim asked a second later, after he'd sat down at his monitors and punched up his options screen. "CBS is getting the shit kicked out of it! What fucking market are *you* watching, Sal?"

"Ummmm . . ." Sal said.

"Ummmm, what?" Jim asked.

"You said . . . CVS."

Jim gaped at Sal. "*What?*"

"You said CVS, didn't you?"

"No, I said C*B*S, Sal."

"Ummmmm . . . I bought . . . CVS calls."

Jim punched up the symbol on his Quotron and saw that instead of being down, he was suddenly up. "Okay . . . So sell 'em." With all seriousness he added, "I had a feeling CVS was going higher."

The calls were flipped for a good return, but from then on CBS was to be referred to as "channel two," and we stuck to trading the drugstore.

There would *always* be an element of chance in this game. Rather than minimize the fact, Jim freely accepted it. To him, coming up with an idea after years of hard work or just plain luck is one thing. Capitalizing on the idea is another. Jim believed that what tipped the odds in your favor was not so much *what* or *why* you were trading, but *how.*

Jim Cramer is first and foremost a trader. His style is a combination of certain disciplines and gut emotion. For most traders, emotion is a negative that forces them to diverge from a considered game plan. In Jim's case, however, his manic personality happened to lend itself perfectly to a technique built on taking advantage of small movements in the marketplace. Couple with this certain "rules" that he learned from years of studying short-term trading patterns, and you have the two basic elements of his success.

Jim knew that stocks rarely go straight up or down without at least a brief turn, and his goal was to dance on that very fine edge of opportunity. To help him in this pursuit, Jim relied on a few technical indicators to determine attractive levels to buy or sell along contrarian lines. His favorite was the "ten-day moving oscillator," a running statistic that assesses whether the market in general is "overbought" or "oversold." At certain depressed levels it became oversold, which just meant it was too late to sell. Likewise, at certain elevated levels it became overbought, or too late to buy.

Along with the ten-day moving oscillator, Jim watched two intraday indicators, the "tick" and the "trin." The tick was merely a cumulative number of stocks that at any given time were being hit down or taken up. The trin, although a slightly more complex equation, also provided a specific data point that showed when a participant should step into or out of the marketplace.

In general, these indicators told Jim what he usually already sensed: that the market was due for a *short-term* bounce or sell-off.

Jim had the stocks he liked or disliked, and he traded accordingly. Whether Candace Bergen liked her Starbucks Grande-Latte-Mocha-Cappuccino-Icy-Thingamajig or Jeff had heard from a reliable industry source that the consumer *wasn't* buying the Starbucks Grande-Latte-Mocha-Cappuccino-Icy-Thingamajig, Jim would watch and wait. If Starbucks was down two points and the market oversold, he might be a buyer. If Starbucks was up two points and the market overbought, he would be a seller.

No matter how much he liked a stock, it was most likely gone if he had a gain.

"Che-*ching!* Che-*ching!*" he would chirp.

It was one of his favorite expressions. There was no better sound than the ringing of the register. Jim had one of the narrowest ranges out there. A stock was a buy at twenty, a sell at twenty-one, and rarely even a hold in between.

Sound simple? Do it thousands of times a day, and you can be James Cramer. To constantly monitor every turn of the market and a given stock, buying on the dips and selling on *any* bounce, requires a special energy. Try it for a few days. Try it for a few hours. He did it every *minute*. I'm not talking about day trading thousand-share lots of a single stock. Jim was buying twenty, thirty, fifty thousand shares of ten different stocks at a time, committing hundreds of millions of dollars and then slipping right back out as quickly as he went in.

To some degree, every mutual or hedge fund must trade actively. In today's marketplace, portfolio managers can't sit on their hands and watch as stocks undergo sizable fluctuations. It is not uncommon for companies to see their share prices go up or down dramatically *every* day. Most funds have accepted that some of the traditional strategies must be adjusted to capitalize on today's faster pace. But the degree to which Jim traded was, by almost any standard, remarkable.

"Turnover" is a statistic occasionally used in the industry that refers to how many times a portfolio manager literally turns over his or her inventory. If during the course of a year a fund buys one stock and sells it, while they buy another and hold it, that's a 50 percent turnover rate. For a pension fund, the figure is generally low, 10 to 20 percent. For a mutual fund, it will be higher, 60 or 70 percent. This means that only a fraction of the positions stay in the fund for even a year.

There are also statistics on the holding periods for stocks, or the average length of time a stock is kept in a portfolio. On average, a pension fund holds a stock for many years. The average time an individual holds a stock is only a few months.

The turnover rate and holding period are designed to give you a feel for the character of a given fund and of the marketplace as a whole. Recently, turnover rates have been increasing and holding periods decreasing. This explains some of the volatility of the last few years. Individuals and funds are, in general, trading in and out of stocks much more than ever before.

While at Cramer & Company, I was often asked what our turnover rate was. I don't think I could have even calculated it. I was then asked what our average holding period was. I never attempted this one, either. Jim turned over half the portfolio in a day, and the holding period might have been better stated in minutes than in months.

When Jim went on CNBC, he would spout about how a "secular change in the consumer" or a "developing trend in this sector" made a company a "great investment for the long term." Our real strategy, however, was all about taking profits *now*. Back at the office, we were supposed to dump stocks after a quick half-point gain. On TV, Jim would tout a stock we owned, but if it moved up, we would sell. The truth was, we rarely cared what happened tomorrow when money could be made today.

Observing Jim's methods, I soon understood what everyone at the firm found so amusing about my answer to Karen's question on my first day at work. A few days, let alone a few months, was long term at Cramer & Company.

Chapter 7

"THIS IS WALL STREET, THIS IS WHAT WE DO"

"NO, I TOLD YOU! I will *not* go on that shit!"

It's 7:30 on a Wednesday morning, and Jim is on the phone with his psychiatrist. Once again the guy is trying to convince him to take medication.

"I'm willing to sit on the couch twice a week, but that's it. I do just fine on three hours sleep. I *like* getting only three hours of sleep. *Fuck* what Karen told you, I *am* calm, for Christ's sake!"

Jim slams the receiver down on the turret and, picking up his fruit cup, resumes staring at his screens.

"It's a penthouse on Fifty-seventh Street, just south of Central Park." Jeff is sitting next to me, his Gucci loafers kicked up on the desk, talking about his apartment. "There's a health club, and a garage in the basement where I keep my BMW."

Jeff's parking bill is nearly equal to the rent I'm paying for my studio.

"This fruit cup has some old, nasty melon in it." Jim tosses his breakfast into the garbage and looks at me. "There's *nothing* nastier than *old* melon! It gets squishy. Honeydew *has* to be fresh or it loses *all* its flavor. That tasted like rotten yogurt."

"Mine did too," Jeff adds.

So now I'm asking Hanover Deli for two new fruit cups.

"And what is up with those *shirts?*" Jim has a revolted look on his face as he eyes the clothes that Clark, Mark, and I are wearing.

"Wednesday Shirt Day," says Mark, smiling, proud at his own creation. The idea was to wear something "fun," as he worded it the day before. Clark and I are dressed in matching green Hawaiian shirts with palm trees on them. We've been outdone by Mark's orange plaid.

"That is so fucking stupid," Jim pronounces with a scowl, assuring that our first Wednesday Shirt Day is also our last.

"*Stu . . . pid!*" Sal chimes in.

Looking discouraged, our head trader returns to checking the market in a host of stocks on the Instinet. The Instinet is a brand of ECN, or electronic communication network. An ECN is an electronic marketplace that functions simply as a conduit for buyers and sellers. We can punch in a symbol and trade any stock without the use of a broker, so long as there is someone else present who chooses to take the other side. ECNs have facilitated round-the-clock action, and are where nearly all before-the-opening or after-the-close orders are executed.

From the moment Mark walks into the office at 6:00 A.M., Jim is trading. There is a function in the Instinet that informs you how many people are "present," or looking at the same stock as you. At the crack of dawn there aren't many others wanting to buy or sell Intel or Cisco. Come 7:00 A.M., when most other traders are just showing up, coffee in hand, Jim is ready to go.

Clark and I have been busy printing out the internal position sheets. Besides trading, he and I are responsible for all this back office work. Trade reconciliation, pricing, printing, stapling. It might not be portfolio management, but if a mistake is made, it can cost just as much as any other blunder. If Jim thinks we own fifty thousand shares of Microsoft when really we have sixty, catastrophe can result. We learn how important our jobs are when we screw up something.

"When is that *God awful* noise going to *stop?*" Jim yells. For the last few days some kind of construction has been going on across the street. Every other second, the sounds of cement trucks and hydraulic lifts fill our cramped space. "Nick, have you called the mayor yet?"

"Yes," I reply. "After putting me on hold for an hour, they told me they couldn't do anything."

"Do they know *who I am?*" Jim screams.

"I told them," I insist.

By 8:30 A.M., the desk has taken all the research calls. Jeff and Jim confer. A semiconductor company, Advanced Micro Devices, missed the Street's profit projections. In addition, a major telco, Southwestern Bell, was downgraded at Goldman Sachs. One of our brokers, Don from Merrill Lynch, has also chosen to push Jim on Cisco. They are reporting quarterly earnings numbers after the close this afternoon, and it's "a screaming buy!"

Jim suggests that the AMD and SBC news is more than enough to have a spillover effect on the rest of the market. The futures, which trade on a "globex," or twenty-four-hour global basis, indicate he is right: They're previewing a weak opening. The foreign indexes have also all been hammered. Jeff agrees, and the two start to strategize on the names they should avoid and those they might buy. Opportunities will arise from stocks that either don't react to the general market or, on the other hand, overreact.

Prices had gone out the previous day at their lowest levels, which Jim saw as a negative technical sign, so we had liquidated most positions that we might otherwise have held. It was an astute call and has left us in good shape. Rather than being forced to average down, we can start fresh.

"Mark? Can I hear where things are?" Jim asks.

Mark repeats what he told Jim five minutes before. "Cisco's down a half, Microsoft's down a quarter, Intel is looking unchanged."

Clark and I begin calling various floor brokers to get indications on the "listed" stocks that we might want to do something in, depending on how they look to open. Listed names are simply stocks that trade on the NYSE. We ask about EMC, IBM, Compaq, and a few others. At 9:26 A.M., four minutes before trading officially starts, the calls flood back in.

The way Jim plays is directly influenced by the structures of the various markets. First, there's the New York Stock Exchange, housed in a big, white building with pillars, at the corner of Wall and Broad in Manhattan. Then there's the Nasdaq, which is an electronic exchange with only a symbolic Times Square location. Trades on the Nasdaq take place at any number of physical locations or simply somewhere out in cyberspace. This difference should tell you something about the two marketplaces.

On the floor of the NYSE, every trade goes through a "specialist" who is responsible for "maintaining a fair and orderly market." What this means is that an experienced and independent authority is in place at a central location, or "post," to keep trading orderly. In addition to the specialist, there are people with titles like "governor" and "reporter," all there to enact an intricate system of checks and balances in regard to strict rules and regulations.

On the Nasdaq there are no specialists, governors, or reporters—only hundreds of competing market makers whose primary goal is to try to figure out what everyone else is doing and make a quick buck trading in and out of the market with an extremely short-term horizon. Market makers are therefore just like any other hyperactive day trader. Their presence makes the Nasdaq the Wild West of the major exchanges.

For these and other reasons, trading on the Nasdaq and trading on the NYSE are two entirely different games. On the Nasdaq, besides keeping track of the various market makers, at any time it might just be easier to use an ECN. With all this in mind, Jim trades the NYSE names himself and chooses to have Mark place Nasdaq orders for him. Mostly, it's good to have a front man like Mark for the kind of gunslinging that Jim might need or want to do here.

"EMC paired on seventy thousand shares. Looking unched," Clark yells out two minutes before the opening. This means that the specialist on the NYSE has cumulative orders of seventy thousand shares to buy, as well as seventy to go. Supply is equal to demand; therefore the stock is going to open where it closed the previous day, unchanged.

"Short ten thousand shares," Jim orders.

"The last tick is a plus," Clark replies.

This means it is a legal short. The "plus tick" rule states that a short seller can't just hit a bid. The idea is that unless you really own shares, you shouldn't be able to come in and cream a stock.

"Two hundred Compaq for sale," I tell Jim, keeping the broker on the wire. "Looking down three-quarters from the last." Compaq is therefore looking "heavy" with sellers and is indicated to open lower.

"Buy ten Compaq," Jim orders, and I relay the directions to the broker.

There is a whole language to trading, spoken in a rushed manner. There can be no saying "Make me an offer" if you want to find a buyer. That will confuse everybody and potentially create an extremely costly mistake. In this marketplace, only a seller can offer, and only a buyer can bid.

If a trader calls me and says, "A hundred for fifty IBM," he is making a $100 bid to buy fifty thousand shares of IBM. If he calls back and says, "Fifty IBM at one," he is offering to sell fifty thousand IBM at $101. "For" means a buyer; "at" means a seller. These terms also indicate price sensitivity. People bidding or offering are in no rush. They are, as Jim always is, trying to squeeze out those extra few pennies.

When traders who are selling want to get more aggressive, they say, "Hit it!" This means hit a bid, rather than offer a stock. If they're on the other side and trying to buy, they say, "Take it!" Take the offer, rather than bid for stock. "Get it in," Jim might shout, pulling his hands toward his body. "I said get rid of it!" he could say two seconds later, pushing his arms away.

Whatever you want to do, you have to say it *fast*.

When the bell rings at 9:30 A.M., it's all hands on deck. Every monitor on the desk comes alive like a slot machine pumped full of quarters. Jim is watching over five hundred stocks, including all the indexes and futures, on his six screens. He's constantly yelling over to Jeff, announcing what he sees.

"The networkers are getting creamed, which makes sense if telco spending will slow. But Cisco is reporting after the close, and it's a layup," Jim reminds Jeff.

"There's no way Cisco doesn't put up a good number," Jeff agrees.

"Sal, get me a market in the April thirty, thirty-five, and forty calls," Jim says. He wants quotes on three different Cisco "calls." Calls are stock options that enable people to make a bet when they think something good is imminent in a particular stock. Calls grant the holder the "right to buy" a stock at a given price (the strike) within a given time period (the expiration month). If the stock price rises above the strike within the time period, the buyer makes money.

"Out of rotation," Jim adds. In options lingo, this means he simply wants quotes on these when available. Because equity options are always based on a stock price, they don't trade until a few minutes *after* that stock opens.

"Mark, buy me ten thousand Cisco. I think this is a good entry point." Jim decides to dive in with the stock down a full point. Sal and I begin fielding the various option quotes and passing them on to him.

"Buy me five hundred of the thirtys at six and a half, five hundred of the thirty-fives at three, and a thousand of the fortys! I'm a half bid for the April fortys!" Jim yells, and Sal and I get to work placing the orders.

"I'm telling you that this Cisco idea of mine will start getting around," Jim declares.

"It's good," Jeff agrees. They understand exactly why it's down, and they also have a catalyst on the immediate horizon to get it back up.

"I know, I know! I'm holding Cisco into the number! I *know* it's a layup! We're holding Cisco into the number! Where do we stand on those calls?" Jim looks at Sal, who picks up a phone to ask the broker what's just been asked of him. Holding something into the number means you intend to let the position ride through a company's earnings announcement.

"A hundred Merck to buy at the market, Morgan Stanley!" Mark yells.

Throughout the trading day, we're inundated with such "order flow"—various brokers calling in customer orders they are working for other large institutional clients. In this case, Morgan Stanley has a customer who wants to buy a hundred thousand shares of Merck. Brokers call us with the hope that we have the other side of the trade; in this case possibly we have Merck stock for sale. If we do, they can collect commissions from both the buy *and* the sale. Their job is easier and more profitable.

The problem with leaking order flow to us is that although we do occasionally provide the other side to keep this info coming, more often we turn around and front-run their orders. Jim can easily deduce that if Morgan Stanley is advertising a buyer of a hundred, the hundred is probably only a fraction of the overall order. The fact that Morgan Stanley said "at the market," meaning this is a market order, is also helpful. They intend to aggressively take any stock that's offered. Numerous times *every* day, such information is used to register a quick hit.

"Take ten thousand Merck." Jim picks up his phone and gives this order to one of his floor brokers. "Fast!"

"Large buyer of Pfizer, Goldman!" Clark yells.

"And ten Pfizer," Jim adds before hanging up. Whenever Goldman Sachs describes an order as "large," or "size," Jim can almost always count on a half a point if he's quick. Remember, this is *institutional* order flow, from customers such as Fidelity, Alliance, and Wellington. It can take one of these mutual fund giants *months* of buying a given stock *every day* to establish a position. Any chance we get to capitalize on our status as a smaller, more nimble hedge fund *must* be taken advantage of.

Mark demonstrates the point to me with an illustration on the Cramer & Company blackboard: a small bird hitching a free ride on the back of an elephant.

"Look at the drugs!" Jim screams, jumping up from his seat. Most of the major drugs, after opening roughly unchanged, are now moving up. Jim's multiple screens are divided into sectors. This way he can quickly assess which groups are being bought and which sold. If money is coming out of one place, it's often heading somewhere else. "*That's* where the money is going!"

"Johnny John is still down a half," Jeff adds. "All the others are starting to run. That's where the money is going, all right."

No sooner is Jim getting the reports back on the MRK and PFE he bought than he's loading up on another ten of each.

"And ten thousand Johnny John, also," Jim says into the phone.

A pigeon lands on the ledge outside one of our two filthy windows and begins cooing.

"Nick," Jim screams, "*shut that fucking thing up!*"

I run over and bang on the glass because the window can't be opened.

"*Shut that fucking thing up!*" Sal screams at me, but the pigeon won't move and continues cooing.

"*Kill* that fucking *rat* bird!" Jim waves a fist in the air, then says into the phone to his broker, "No, I *wasn't* talking to you! Why would I tell *you* to kill a fucking bird? What have I done in Johnny John?"

I keep banging on the glass, trying to get the pigeon to fly away. It's obviously lived in New York for a long time—it remains unfazed.

"Look at Cisco!" Jim shrieks. Though the stock fell precipitously for a few minutes after the opening bell, it's suddenly catching a bid. Jim sees all the market makers on his Level Two screen trying to buy. A Level Two screen is where you can watch everyone jockey for position in a Nasdaq name. If a stock is for sale, or going down, all the market makers are on the offer. If it is to buy, or going up, they all switch to the bid side. Next to the quantity and the price are acronyms like GSCO (Goldman Sachs), MLCO (Merrill Lynch), MSCO (Morgan Stanley), and SBSH (Salomon Smith Barney).

Cisco is down only seven-eighths. Then three-quarters.

"Mark, buy ten thousand more Cisco. And get in ten Mr. Softie, also!" Jim loves to call Microsoft Mr. Softie. He likes to say the name so much he often trades it just to do that.

"You offered me five hundred of the thirtys at a half, and you're going to sell me five hundred at a half!" Sal is yelling at a broker who has backed away from a quote, having seen the same movement that Jim saw: upward.

"Who the fuck is that?" Jim stands up and leans toward Sal. "Who the fuck is that fading on a firm quote?"

Jim's trading lines are ringing with his newest buys in MRK and PFE, so Clark and I quickly pick them up. We're both shouting to Jim his new totals and averages as he screams at Sal.

"All or none! If you want to play on *my street*, it's *all or none!*"

"No, two-fifty will *not* cut it," Sal goes on.

"No order! No order!" Jim slams a hand down on top of the monitor between him and Sal, who instantly relays the cancellation.

The broker gives us the "out," which means nothing done, and then decides to offer us all five hundred of the calls he wouldn't sell us for a half at three-quarters.

"I'm not going to pay up, or chase *any*thing," Jim declares.

When you're trading like he does, every penny counts, so this offer just pisses him off more.

"Fuck you!" Jim shouts. Before Sal can hang up, Jim grabs the receiver and yells into it, "I can't do business with a fucking lightweight!" He throws the phone in the garbage, and Sal pulls it out as ten different option lines ring.

Cisco is down only five-eighths now.

"Sell the ten Cisco we just bought," Jim tells Mark.

Mark is still on the phone, trying to get a Microsoft report, so he tells Clark to do it. I'm fielding another one of Jim's lines, taking down the newest Johnny John buy. Sal's frantically looking for a napkin because his receiver is covered with old melon.

At 9:45 the futures hit a level of support and start to spike. Jim scans his monitors for any tech names that haven't bounced.

"Morgan Stanley just turned seller of Merck," Mark relays.

"Goldman with size Pfizer to go," Clark adds.

Jim picks up one of his lines and gives a floor broker ten thousand Merck and Pfizer to sell. "Just hit it, fast!" He wants to be sure his broker beats Goldman and Morgan in placing these orders.

"The money's going back into tech!" Jim screams, and Jeff agrees. Jim lifts his receiver again before it has touched the turret and buys back the ten EMC he sold short on the opening.

"Johnny John is up a half a point," Jeff adds. Before he can finish the sentence, Jim hits another wire and tells one of his guys to sell that, too. The next second he's leaning over his terminal, pointing both phones at Mark.

"Buy five thousand Intel . . . no, make that *ten* Intel . . . and buy ten thousand *more* Mr. Softie. What's wrong with Sunny Micro?" Jim looks at Jeff, who instantly picks up the phone and starts calling the Merrill Lynch analyst to find out. It's down two points, far more than the rest of the group. Before Jeff can finish dialing, Sunny Micro starts to turn, following the futures, and there's no time to check.

"Buy ten thousand Sunny Micro!" Jim yells at Mark. "Now!"

"We're done on the thirty-fives and the fortys, Jim." By this point, Sal has taken a report on the Cisco options we did manage to buy.

"Five hundred of the thirty-fives and a thousand of the fortys?" Jim asks.

"Yes."

"Sal, did you buy that shirt from the *Sears* catalogue?" Jim sneers. Sal is wearing a blue and red candy striper's shirt. We would never see it again. "Wednesday Shirt Day . . . That is *so fucking stupid!*"

"I wasn't playing Wednesday Shirt Day," Sal mutters.

Jim turns toward his head trader. "Mark, sell ten thousand Bristol Myers."

"We never bought any Bristol Myers," Mark replies.

"We own the calls," Jim corrects Mark impatiently, aggravated by the delay. Technically, by owning the calls we have the right to buy the stock but don't actually own it.

"So sell it *short?*" Mark asks for clarification. Mark knows that according to the SEC rule book, selling stock you don't already own (even if you *do* own the call options) must be marked and executed as a short sale.

"You are confusing me with someone who gives a shit. Just *sell* it! I said hit the fucking bid!" adds Jim, not interested in wasting time over petty semantics. Skirting the "plus tick" rule in this case won't necessarily make us a lot of extra money, but in Jim's eyes, the rule is still an unenforceable annoyance. "And don't *ever* ask me that again!"

"Nothing going on in Sun Micro," Jeff interrupts after hanging up his phone.

"So what have I done?" Jim asks Mark. Mark has been trying to get a report from Goldman Sachs for the last few minutes. The stock has bounced a quarter of a point since Jim gave the order. "Mark? What the fuck have I done in Sun Micro?"

"Can I *please* hear something?" Mark asks the broker.

Jim has a knee on his chair, and with both hands he pulls at his hair. The tufts stand out like horns. His face is quickly turning bright red as he looks over at Jeff. Jeff stares with an open mouth, conveying that Mark has done something *very* wrong.

"Can you *please* fuck me up the ass?" Jim yells at Mark. "Can you *please* just fuck me up the ass!!!!"

"Ten thousand SUNW at an average of fifty-two and a half," Mark tells Jim, relieved to finally get the report.

"Noooooo!!!" whines Jim, waving his arms in the air. "It was offered at a quarter when I came in!"

"Ten thousand shares, Jim. The stock was being taken." Mark is maintaining that the report isn't really that bad.

"Who's fucking side are you on?" Jim asks. "Buy another ten."

"Bear Stearns has five thousand of the Cisco fortys to buy, Jim," yells Sal. "They're paying three-quarters!"

"Sold your ten J&J," Clark pipes in.

"Do you want a quote in the Cisco April thirty calls?" I ask Jim. The broker who earlier faded on a half offering and tried to get us to pay three-quarters still feels like playing.

It's almost 10:30 A.M., and the trading wires are still ringing off the hook. We're all standing up now, fielding the calls and telling brokers to "turn off" anything we don't absolutely need to be hearing.

"I still want to know if they're working any *big* orders!" Jim tells us all before turning to Sal. "Sell five hundred of the Cisco fortys at seven-eighths."

"Three-quarter bid," Sal reiterates.

"I *heard* you. I said *offer* them!" Jim glares in Sal's direction and then looks at Clark. "Sell five Merck and five Pfizer."

Clark gets to work.

"Bought your Microsoft," Mark informs him. "Ten more at fifty-one and an eighth."

"Jim." I want to ask him again about the Cisco thirty calls.

"No!" Jim glares at me. "I told that guy *nothing done!!!* Fucking *lightweight!!!*"

"Leave it alone," I say into the phone.

"What's my average on the twenty Mr. Softie?" Jim asks.

"Fifty-one," Clark yells. "No. Fifty-one and an eighth."

"I know it's hard to average *two* lots of ten," Jim says acidly.

The futures have topped out by this point, and the market is almost unchanged for the day.

"The news is still bad," says Jim, thinking aloud. "I don't believe for a minute we've seen the end of the selling."

"AMD *did* miss," Jeff agrees, "and that SBC downgrade didn't just go away."

"What's my average in Sunny Micro?" Jim asks.

"Fifty-two and a half," Clark replies. "You did your second lot of ten at the same price, a half."

"Who *fucked* us on the Sunny Micro?" Jim looks at Mark. Now he's gotten two reports, both of which he believes were too high.

"Goldman sold me the first ten, then shorted me the second lot," Mark explains. The Goldman Sachs market maker has made his spread on the first ten thousand shares. The second lot still needs to be bought back. He sold ten thousand shares he did not yet own.

"I suppose you think he did us a favor?" Jim asks.

"Do I think he did us a favor?"

"Excellent. You heard the fucking question, now *answer* it!"

"Well . . ."

"*Fuck* those guys. Call Merrill and buy me twenty thousand shares!"

"Now call Merrill?" Mark stalls.

"Is there a fucking echo in here?" Jim asks. "*Whose side are you on?*"

Mark picks up the wire and talks the Merrill market maker into shorting us twenty thousand shares of Sun Micro. Once again, the market maker sold stock they do not yet own.

"Okay, you're done," Mark says. "Makes forty thousand shares."

"Call Lehman and buy twenty thousand shares!" Jim orders.

"Jim," Mark pleads, understanding exactly what Jim is trying to do.

"*This is Wall Street,*" Jim says, glaring across the desk at his head trader and speaking slowly in a condescending tone, as if trying to explain something to a two-year-old. "*This is what we do.*"

Mark picks up the phone and talks the Lehman market maker into shorting us twenty thousand more shares of Sun Micro. We have now forced three different market makers to short us stock. Three separate people, therefore, are trying to buy SUNW at the same time to flatten their positions. Each respective market maker sees his competitors trying to buy, and all inevitably become concerned, not knowing what the sudden rush is about. Only Cramer & Company knows that answer—Jim has caused a classic short squeeze.

He grins as he watches his Level Two screen. Goldman Sachs, Merrill Lynch, and Lehman are all on the bid side, driving SUNW up in violent fashion. Mark refers to this practice as "machine gunning," because he hits every market maker at once. It's not something he likes to do, but it gets Jim off his back.

"Now, start offering the stock out in the box," Jim instructs. The "box" is the Instinet. Mark does as he's told, and we quickly peel off all sixty thousand shares, selling back to the market makers what we bought from them a point cheaper thirty seconds earlier.

Causing such a squeeze is always good for a quick buck at the expense of the market makers.

"Sell the ten Compaq I bought on the open," Jim yells to Clark the instant he tells one of his brokers to sell his last five thousand MRK and PFE. As soon as the phone is out of his hand, he leans over his monitors. "Mark, seriously, whose side are you on?"

"Sold your five hundred Cisco April fortys at seven-eighths," Sal interjects.

"Mark?" Jim asks.

"Jim?" Sal says.

"I heard you!" Jim snaps. "Mark?"

Our secretary walks in to ask Jim what he wants for lunch. It's almost 11:00 A.M., after all, and Jim can get furious if his lunch is late. Smiling, she says, "Hanover has your favorite special today—"

"What?" Jim looks over at her.

"Hanover has your steamed—"

Jim throws a pencil at her head.

"Get the *fuck* away from me, *now!*" he screams.

Every trading wire suddenly rings as Mark attempts to find out where we sold the Bristol Myers while Clark tries to get rid of the Compaq and I tell the secretary to order Jim the usual and not take it personally.

"No, he *wasn't* trying to hit you," I assure her. "He was just . . . I don't know." I give up.

Sal's being bid a buck by Bear Stearns for the five hundred Cisco forty calls we still own, and Jim pushes his hands away from his body to signal that Sal should sell them. The futures fade once again.

"Sal, sell the five hundred Cisco April thirty-fives we bought, also," Jim says.

"Mark, hit the half bid to get rid of the twenty Mr. Softie. Sell the Mr. Softie! Sell the Mr. Softie! Sell the Mr. Softie!" he shouts, waving his arms in the air. "Sell the last ten Cisco! Did you sell the Mr. Softie, Mr. Softie, Mr. Softie?"

He grabs one of his ringing phones and his face turns tomato red as he screams into it, "*This is unacceptable!* There is *no fucking way* I am taking *that* report!" The broker sold Merck an eighth lower than he should have.

"And *what* the *fuck* has been done in *Intel?*" Jim looks at Mark, who is trying to explain to Goldman Sachs, Merrill Lynch, and Lehman that he *didn't* just "plug them," which in fact is exactly what we had just done.

"I SAID TWENTY FUCKING INTEL!!! I SAID TWENTY FUCKING INTEL!!!" Jim climbs on top of the trading desk and starts jumping up and down. I wonder if the desk is going to hold. "I SAID TWENTY FUCKING INTEL!!! I SAID TWENTY FUCKING INTEL!!!"

The day isn't even *half* over.

An hour later, trading has calmed down and I ask Mark for permission to take my first bathroom break, which he grants. No sooner am I back than Jeff leans toward me to say, "I got the apartment on Fifty-seventh Street because I was able to write a check for the first year's rent *on the spot*. Did I mention the health club?"

"Yes, you did."

"What about the garage?"

"Yes, you mentioned the garage."

"I can look at Central Park, work out, and get in my BMW without *ever* leaving the building," he explains. "By the way, can you call the Cisco IR department and get me their conference call info? Think of that: if it's snowing out, or if it's, like, a hundred and ten degrees? To go from my air-conditioned health club to my air-conditioned car up to my air-conditioned apartment? What's better than that?"

"Nothing!" I reply, picking up an outside line. I get the number from a Bloomberg terminal and dial the Cisco headquarters.

Within a minute the investor relations representative is on the phone. As I ask her for the phone number of the conference call, I hear Jim screaming in the background. "What the fuck is going on out there? What the fuck is going on out there?"

I stick a finger in one ear and crouch under the desk to continue my phone conversation. Whether listening to a conference call, speaking with a company representative, or calling Hanover Deli, this is how I did it.

"This is *unacceptable!*" Jim roars.

"What the *hell* is happening over there?" the rep asks.

"Nothing," I reply and ask again for the conference call number.

"Fuck this!" Jim finally says. The construction going on across the street is growing louder by the second. Since the two filthy windows in the trading room don't open, Jim sprints into Jeff's office, pulls open that window, and starts yelling down to the street, seven floors below.

"Shut the fuck up! Shut the fuck up!"

He's leaning so far out the window it looks as if he might fall.

"*You* shut the fuck up!" comes a voice from above. "They can't hear you, you fucking idiot! *You* shut the fuck up!"

"Fuck you!" Jim turns his head up. He can't find the culprit. Frustrated, he pulls himself back inside.

"You." Jim points at me with both hands as he returns to his place at the head of the trading desk. I lift my head up as I jot down the conference call number. "Strap on some balls and go tell them to shut the fuck up!"

I glance at Jeff, who has his Gucci loafers kicked up again. He gives me a look that says, "Go, already!"

Reluctantly, I run downstairs to the construction site. I consider going next door and just getting some coffee to kill time, but when I look up toward our offices, there are five faces in Jeff's window, staring down at me. Once I see some bills change hands between Jim and Jeff, I know I can't turn away without trying.

Fifty huge guys are working away. Thinking that whoever doesn't get too dirty is probably the foreman, I walk up to the one wearing a clean hard hat. He's twice my size and clenches an oversized hammer.

"Excuse me!" I shout.

"What?!" he yells, looking at my green Hawaiian shirt. "Who are you?!"

"I work up there!" I point. "And I was wondering . . . could you *not* make so much noise?"

"What?!" He can't hear me over the cement trucks and hydraulic lifts.

"*Can you quiet the fuck down?!*" I scream.

The guy looks at me as if I'm out of my mind.

When I go back upstairs, the noise as loud as when I left, Jim has a thoroughly frustrated look on his face and shakes his head in disappointment.

"You just cost me twenty bucks," he says.

"I tried."

"I thought you could pull it off."

"I didn't," Jeff laughs, with Jim's twenty in his hand.

The only thing that distracts Jim is that it's close to 12:30 and his lunch hasn't yet arrived.

"*Where* is my lunch?" Jim asks, trying to remain calm because the secretary has *finally* stopped crying from her earlier brush with flying lead.

By 3:30 in the afternoon, Cramer & Company has traded almost five million shares. A quarter of a billion dollars' worth of stock has been bought and sold. It's a good day, and we're up close to $500,000. That's on top of paying out $150,000 in commissions to the Street. The fund is essentially flat, positionwise, from where we came in that morning. The market is selling off, precisely as Jim thought it would, and it looks as if prices will be going out at the lows once again.

Clark and I are starting to recap with our various brokers so we're not in the office until 8:00 that evening. Hanover is good for breakfast and lunch, but by dinner it starts getting old. Mark is doing damage control with the various market makers we plugged over the course of the day, so that maybe tomorrow they will trade with us again. Sal is surfing online for a new shirt. Jim and Jeff are sitting back at the desk, watching their monitors.

"The market's going lower," Jim says.

"Looks that way," Jeff agrees.

"What's left Cisco?" Jim looks over at Sal.

"We still have the thousand April forty calls," he replies. After buying the thousand options that morning, which is the equivalent of owning a hundred thousand shares of stock (since each "contract" is worth a hundred shares), we flipped them to Bear Stearns when they were a buyer. By midafternoon the calls had "come in," or gone down, with Cisco stock and the rest of the market. Jim then bought them back where he did in the first place, a half.

"I'm holding them into the number; it's a layup," he says again.

"There's no way Cisco doesn't put up a good number," Jeff concludes.

"Watch the stock on the close. That's when everyone else will catch on to what I'm thinking," Jim goes on.

"I'm watching," says Jeff.

Fifteen minutes before the closing bell at 4:00 P.M., Cisco is doing exactly what Jim expected. It's bouncing against the tide. While the rest of the tech-heavy Nasdaq market is selling off, Cisco is up an eighth. Five minutes before the bell, it's up a half.

"Where are the Cisco April fortys?" Jim asks Sal.

"Buck and an eighth bid, offered at a quarter."

"Buck and an eighth bid?" Jim looks at Jeff.

"Do what you want."

"Sell 'em," Jim decides. "Che-*ching!* Che-*ching!*"

At 4:32, as Clark, Mark, Sal, and I sort through the hundreds of trade tickets from the day, the secretary approaches Jim, who is compulsively scanning the headlines on his multiple screens. She has a message from his psychiatrist: He called a prescription in for Jim to the Duane Reed pharmacy on Water Street.

"I thought I told you to *stay the fuck away from me!*" Jim screams. This time she retreats as he reaches for a paperweight.

"I said, I will not take that shit!"

Suddenly Cisco's quarterly number comes across the scrolling news tape. It is three cents ahead of expectations.

"Fuck!" Jim yells from behind his monitors. "Fuck! Fuck! Fuck! I *knew* it was a layup!"

"The market was getting hit," says Jeff, trying to calm him down.

"But I *knew* it was a layup! I *knew!*" Jim yanks on his hair. He looks down at his Level Two screen to see buyers in the various ECNs tripping over themselves to get the stock in. ISLD (Island), BRUT (Brut), and INCA (Instinet) all pop up on his monitor with twenty, fifty, and a hundred thousand shares to buy. Since it's after the official close, the ECNs are where the action is.

The Nasdaq futures jump twenty points, then thirty. Tomorrow will be a big day for tech, and Cramer & Company is not in shape to capitalize on the move. The calls that Jim flipped for a buck and an eighth will open in the morning at three. The $200,000 that could have been made now becomes the focus, instead of the money already in the register.

The Cisco revenue numbers come across the tape. The Dow Jones headline states that Cisco is a few hundred million *shy* of estimates. Jim glances down to see the stock start to fall. Over a hundred thousand shares are being offered for *sale* through the various ECNs. The Nasdaq futures are in free fall, down twenty, thirty, even forty points.

"I knew it was too risky to hold Cisco into the number!" Jim starts screaming, ecstatic. "I knew it! I knew it!"

"Obviously most of the good news was factored in," Jeff adds.

"That *fucking idiot* Don! How many people did he *kill* with that idea?" Jim is picking up his phone and dialing Don's number. Don is the Merrill Lynch broker who suggested the name that morning. "You don't get off scot-free *fucking up* like *that!* What a *stupid fucking idea* that guy had! He's off this account, that *stupid fuck!!!*"

"You tell him," Jeff says.

The Dow Jones news tape scrolls by with the latest headline. It's a correction. Cisco's revenues were, in fact, $200 million *better* than expected. The previous headline was a misprint. Jim drops his phone onto the trading desk. Cisco is suddenly to buy. The Nasdaq futures are jumping once again.

"*Fuck, fuck, fuck!*" Jim screams. He's standing behind his monitors, a pained expression all over his face. His shirt is untucked and he reaches underneath an already loosened tie for more air, his forehead breaking out in sweat.

"*MOTHER FUCKER!!!* I KNEW IT WAS A LAYUP!!! I KNEW IT WAS A LAYUP!!! I KNEW IT WAS A LAYUP!!! *MOTHER FUCKER!!!*"

Jim lifts a monitor, raises it high over his head, and lets it fall to the floor. The glass shatters, and smoke rises from its hollow center.

By now I know why he keeps a stack of new parts behind his desk. I can replace a screen in seconds flat. It's important, however, never to go in to do the job too early. This time, I can tell he's not done yet. Jim kicks over a hard drive next to him and starts jumping up and down on top of it. Then he tries to lift the *whole* trading desk. It doesn't budge. Determined, he tries again. His head looks as if it's about to explode. He can't lift it, and collapses back into his chair, exhausted.

Chapter 8

DISCRETIONARY DISCLOSURE

TRADING EVERY MINUTE for quarters and halves to net a few cents per trade might not be how most money managers go about their business, but this was how Jim operated every day. What he loved to do most was trade, trade, and trade. He consistently made money this way. There were times when everything seemed to be going wrong, and Jim's abilities and energy on the desk literally saved the firm.

Jim understood that such an approach created other benefits. One of them was that Cramer & Company gave out huge commissions to all of the largest Wall Street brokerage houses. Some would argue this is a cost best minimized, but not Jim. His strategy was if you can make money trading while simultaneously paying the Street, there would be a certain return. It's in everyone's best interest to see you do well.

I once asked Jim about these massive brokers' fees. Why would I, as an individual investor, pay less than Jim Cramer, who traded millions of shares every day? If I wanted to buy a thousand shares of a stock, I could pay any discount broker $8 to make the trade. Jim, on the other hand, paid his brokers a flat rate of 6 cents a share on NYSE trades. That meant the same thousand shares (not that Jim ever traded only a thousand shares) cost him $60 in broker fees.

"You can buy your clothes from the Sears catalogue," he replied, looking at Sal, "or you can go to Barney's." He pinched his own cashmere sweater. "You get what you pay for."

One year our options business lagged behind only Fidelity and Alliance, two of the biggest mutual funds on the Street. They manage hundreds of billions of dollars, and their commissions are based on a cumulative of hundreds of funds, many of which are individually larger in assets than Cramer & Company. On an absolute basis, we almost matched these guys. On a relative basis, therefore, these numbers are all the more remarkable. This obviously made us one of the top accounts on Wall Street.

Every year the *McLagan Report* presents data on the commissions paid out by various institutions. All the major brokerage houses buy the report to see who the biggest accounts are and where they stand. If Cramer paid out a total of $50 million in broker fees, but a certain brokerage house received only $5,000, you can bet this broker will do whatever it takes to get a larger piece of the pie. The *McLagan Report* ensured that Cramer & Company had brokers willing to do nearly anything for us.

What Jim expected, although expensive, wasn't really that complicated.

One day a stock we owned suddenly plummeted shortly after lunch. Jeff called around to discover that First Boston had just downgraded it. Before Jeff even had a chance to explain to this broker the grievous error he just committed, Jim was leaning over his monitors, screaming at the top of his lungs.

"I want to talk to that fucking guy, *right now!!!*"

He found the line Jeff was on and jumped in.

"*Shut the fuck up* and *listen to me,* you *stupid* fucking *idiot!*" Jim yelled as Jeff moved the phone away from his ear. He was getting Jim in stereo. "*I'm* going to tell *you* what your job is. I don't want you to think. I don't want you to even try and use your fucking head. All I pay you *too much fucking money for* is to pick up the *goddamn phone* when there is news! I just want you to *pick up* the *goddamn phone* and call me—call *me*—before you call *anyone* else!"

The primary asset any premium brokerage house offers its clients is research. All the major houses have analysts who cover most of the publicly traded companies, and Wall Street constantly looks to them to interpret events. A call from a brokerage house can have as great an impact on a stock's price as a company press release. Often, it's less important to hear the news itself than to hear what some of these people are saying about it. Jim didn't care whether an analyst was ultimately right in his or her opinion. He just wanted to take advantage of the closest thing to a sure bet in the stock market today: the short-term effect any commentary might have.

If one of the major brokerage houses, be it Bear Stearns, Morgan Stanley, Merrill Lynch, or First Boston, upgraded or downgraded a stock, *we* were to be the first call. This was usually done in the "morning meeting," where all the various research calls from analysts were discussed with the "sales force." The sales force consisted of the brokers whose job it was to deal directly with the clients.

The morning call was designed to get the news out sooner than anyone could run with it, since an 8:00 A.M. upgrade was an hour and a half before the opening. For the same reason, publicly traded companies tried to limit important news releases, such as earnings, to nonmarket hours. The idea was also to give people a chance to evaluate any development prior to trading on it.

All this changed with the birth of the ECN. Now the market is *always* open. Down time has been eliminated. No matter what hour of the day it was, Jim insisted on being the initial call from a broker. If we weren't the first firm to be selling on a downgrade or buying on an upgrade, someone's head would roll.

As the First Boston broker learned, it was best if we were phoned as an analyst stepped to the podium for a morning or afternoon call. This is often the way analysts at brokerage firms give their news to the sales force. They talk over a PA system to everyone, and then the brokers go out with the call. This usually allows a slight lag time between the analysts' speaking and the news going public.

At Cramer & Company, we wanted to listen *as* they spoke. Brokers were expected to merely turn on their speakerphones. When the technology analyst at Goldman Sachs spoke about a conversation he or she just had with Sun Microsystems or EMC, we heard it firsthand. As soon as words like "disappointing" or "above expectations" came out of the analyst's mouth, we got to work. By the time anyone at home hears from CNBC about a report some brokerage house issued, all the best accounts have already adjusted their portfolios accordingly and moved on.

The next time First Boston made an intraday call, it was obvious that Jim's message had got through loud and clear. As soon as the analyst was about to open his mouth to everyone on the sales floor, the broker called us. When we heard that the analyst had something incrementally positive to say, Jim bought as much stock as he could before it started to get around. When the price was up a quarter, then three-eighths, we had already acquired our position. As the rest of the Street heard the news, we were sitting pretty. By the time Maria Bartiromo or David Faber started talking about it on CNBC, Cramer & Company was selling.

Sometimes we didn't even have to be the first to hear what analysts said. We knew beforehand what they were going to say.

Good brokers chat with the analysts at their firm as often as they can—on the sales floor, on the elevator, in the cafeteria. They're asking about their kids, about their weekend plans, and about order backlog and sales expectations. If anything changed, brokers were expected to come to us with this information. Some accounts might not want to hear a guy speculating that an analyst has changed his or her tune, but we did. We encouraged this. And I'm not talking about whether the analyst was going to the Jersey shore instead of the Hamptons.

At Cramer & Company, we also spoke directly to a long list of brokerage house analysts. All these analysts see account rankings, just as the brokers do. It's also easy for them to find out what holdings these accounts have in their portfolio. They know who they need to keep happy, and how. For the best accounts, like Cramer & Company, part of this brokerage house service means keeping clients apprised of changes regarding companies under coverage. Analysts always let some people know information *before* a formal report is released.

When I began doing research at Cramer & Company, I learned this firsthand. A prominent analyst invited me out to dinner, and Jim was thrilled. But before I went to the Tribeca Grill and ordered seared yellow fin tuna, I was to get another lesson from Jim.

"The reason it's good to go *out* with these people," Jim explained, "is that the analysts are safe to talk."

He was right. This analyst told me "sales had slumped recently" at one of the major home-goods stores, which concerned him greatly. He went on to say that his rating was currently under review. Cramer & Company shorted a hundred thousand shares of Lowes by the time the downgrade arrived a few days later.

Another time I met a Smith Barney analyst, whom I'd been talking to on the phone for a few months, at Chelsea Billiards for a game of pool. After a few beers, Joe told me that he had just visited a certain corporate headquarters and found that fundamentals at the company "appear to be turning around and the long-term prospects are improving."

"You guys have a hold rating on that stock, don't you?" I asked, sinking the six-ball in the corner pocket.

"For now," he replied, polishing off his third Heineken.

Before I could congratulate myself, the analyst set me straight.

"Listen, Sherlock, just remember one thing. If you're going to buy it, buy it with us. We get a cut of every trade you do in the stocks we cover."

Thus there was a quantifiable reason that such information was "leaked" to good clients like Cramer & Company. This senior analyst received a direct kickback from getting Cramer & Company to traffic in the stocks his company covered. Joe helped me to make money, and I was expected to return the favor. By the time the stock was upgraded from a hold to a strong buy, Cramer & Company had bought fifty thousand shares. All the trades were placed with Smith Barney.

For the few times I managed to flush out such a call ahead of time, Jim and Jeff managed to get *far* more. My efforts were merely a reflection of having learned from the best. For each analyst I had to pester constantly, those guys had five pestering *them*. Everyone knew it was Jim and Jeff running the show. Why talk to me when you can go straight to those who write the checks? Upgrades, downgrades, even impending news articles. Nothing was beyond a player's reach.

Besides CNBC, there are a few printed business publications that can trigger moves in the marketplace. The most obvious is the *Wall Street Journal.* The *Journal* has a column called "Heard on the Street" that is almost guaranteed to push a mentioned stock. Likewise, if you find your biggest holding raved about on the cover of Saturday morning's *Barron's,* you can bet Monday will be profitable. *Business Week* is also very influential. Discover that one of your stocks is mentioned in a negative light in *Business Week* when it hits the newsstands on Friday, and it can ruin a weekend long before you have the chance to cry, "sell!"

On several occasions we were told ahead of time what would be printed in these publications. Usually our source was a brokerage house analyst who had been questioned by a reporter and then called us. The journalist would need to talk to a reputable Wall Street expert and would happen to reveal to the analyst what the article was about. Other times a reporter might just lead the discussion, asking questions that indicated the tone of an upcoming article. *Barron's* wanted a quote from Morgan Stanley about how overvalued a certain Internet stock is, or the *Journal* needed Merrill Lynch to tell them why some small paper company will likely get bought out. After the analyst told them what they wanted to hear, the analyst told us what the next day's headline would be.

Sometimes we didn't know where the leak came from, only that it was worth listening to. There were calls from certain people you just *knew* to listen to and *not* ask about. One Thursday a broker gave us a heads up on a *Business Week* story. We didn't need to hear anything more, because the day before, that broker had known what was coming out in a Heard on the Street column.

For a few months it seemed like *all* of Wall Street knew what was going to be in *Business Week*. On Friday morning a mentioned name would go up or down accordingly, but, almost always, punching up a simple chart showed that the day before it had *already* moved. To know if someone heard something ahead of time, just look at a daily chart. Plenty of times stocks spike *before* a news item is officially released.

Being a Wall Street insider means getting the news before it's news. With a lot of money and a little effort, the system is easily manipulated. If you believe the everyday investor gets the same level of service as someone like Jim Cramer, you probably should stop trading now. The little guy might have a gripe with all this, but most of Wall Street sees no problem with such discretionary disclosure. One timely call could make our day, week, or even month.

Chapter 9

HOUSE OF CARDS

PAYING OUT MILLIONS of dollars in commissions yielded all kinds of benefits, not the least of which was the chance to participate in initial public offerings—the new issues of a company's stock that an investment bank sells to the public for the first time. Hot deals go out to the firm's best customers and open at a premium, giving an instant gain to those fortunate few. Like early calls, IPOs are available only to the Wall Street heavyweights who are a brokerage house's best friends. I personally kept the figures on the IPO contribution to Cramer & Company, and it added up to 5 percent a year to our returns. This was a *huge* benefit to the bottom line.

When a private company decides to go public, it hires an investment bank to oversee the transition. All the major brokerage houses have investment banking divisions. A valuation is placed on the actual assets, intellectual property, and goodwill before, for example, a fair price of $20 a share is determined for a company. Everyone gets all jazzed up, as people always do when a company is new, and by the time that stock opens for its first trade, buyers are willing to pay $30 a share. Bingo! Cramer & Company just made a quick ten points on the few thousand shares it received at the IPO price.

There have obviously been IPOs that reward the long-term holder. After all, every great stock was brought into the public sector at some point. Microsoft, McDonald's, WalMart, all of these made very wealthy people out of the investors who were smart and patient enough to hold on to them. The truth is, however, that these are extremely rare exceptions. As Jim taught me, the very process of bringing a new company public today is rife with charade, so much so that Jim insisted on cashing out of every IPO as soon as possible.

When I arrived at Cramer & Company there was a woman named Betsy who worked as syndicate manager (IPOs are put together by a syndicate, or group of investment banks; thus the term). Betsy was tall and thin and had an outgoing, warm personality. Jim described her to me as "not having too much upstairs, but *great* legs."

When Betsy inevitably missed a deal that could have made us money, not even her physical attributes could save her from Jim's wrath. Someone happened to mention to Jim, "Boy, can you believe that deal Smith Barney brought today? Up three hundred percent by the first trade?" After the monitor crashed to the floor, Betsy was told to find a new job, and I had another responsibility.

At the end of that day, Jim called me over to talk and actually asked me to take a seat. Usually, he threw information at me and I was on my way. Jim was *always* "completely jammed," as he worded it, and trust me, you didn't want to be responsible for slowing the guy down. If he was asking me to sit, it had to be serious.

"IPOs are the way the brokerage houses pay back their customers," Jim explained. "Their investment banking divisions make money underwriting the deal, we make money when it opens at a premium, and the only people fucked are the idiots who hold on longer than the initial print. *Your* job," he added, "will be to act as if you love these pieces of shit."

The first step in all this was keeping track of the IPO deals on the horizon and trying to figure out which would be the hottest. When we were "playing the calendar," as we called this process, it wasn't appropriate for us to go in on all the deals. Genuine interest would be discerning. I started by scanning the schedule and networking to hear the buzz. If the latest Internet stock was on everybody else's radar screen, it was on mine. We didn't care one bit whether or not these companies were truly sound. All I tried to ascertain was the premium the first trade would generate.

Once I picked a favorite, I was to speak to our broker and place an initial order. For instance, when Amazon and Netscape were about to go public, I requested five hundred thousand shares of a five-million-share offering, far more than I ever hoped to get. In this way such deals became "oversubscribed." Everyone on the Street did the same thing. One hundred accounts all asking for 10 percent of a deal makes it ten times oversubscribed. This makes an IPO "hot"—routine and misleading inflated orders from institutions, all ultimately hoping to get a few shares.

Finding the hottest deals to go after and putting in for an enormous number of shares was only the beginning. I also went to the "road show," as we called the long, boring lunches at a local hotel, often the Waldorf, Palace, or Regency. These are essentially infomercials during which the company's CEO and CFO carry on for an hour about how great their company is. Everything is packaged for a quick sale. The most biased individuals, company managers, paint the most optimistic case scenario.

At the road show, it honestly didn't matter if I read the prospectus or even listened to a word they said. The only thing I had to do was pick up my nametag, because attendance was taken. If the meeting was at the Palace, I might stay and eat. (It was the only hotel with decent food.) Occasionally I would get a nametag and sneak next door to pick up another tag from a different IPO road show. I ran all over midtown, collecting nametags. Four in one day was my record.

Next I called the analyst at the brokerage house and told him or her how *very* interested I *really* was in the new company. I said that I believed this company would make a great "long-term" investment.

These analysts had some pull with the investment bankers that eventually added up all the various factors to "allocate" the deal. This allocation would be based on a cumulative score of sorts:

Wants 10 percent of the deal, just like everybody else? Check.

Went to the road show? Check.

Called the analyst and acted as if he really loved the stock? Check.

Paid our brokerage house millions in commissions this year? Check.

Of course this factor was the most important one, and why the little guy can never expect to get in on hot IPOs.

The final hoop we had to jump through in this whole process was known as an "aftermarket order." The underwriters, in an attempt to hold us to our word, wanted Cramer & Company to commit to buying the stock *after* it started trading. If you *really* are *very* interested, and deserve your five thousand shares of the IPO priced at $20, you should promise to buy fifty thousand more shares wherever the thing opens, be it $50 or $500.

Take a typical "hot" deal. I get five thousand shares of an IPO priced at $20 that we think is going to open for trading at $50. I want it *so* much that I agree to buy another fifty thousand at *any* price. I therefore wholeheartedly agree with the investment bank that the IPO is a legitimate and valuable company.

Nearly all of the major investment banks made us commit to aftermarket orders, and they kept score. The investment bankers went to their brokerage house's trading desk to make sure that if Cramer & Company committed to buy in the aftermarket,

Cramer & Company bought in the aftermarket. This was their way of making sure hot deals stayed hot. If we didn't buy in the aftermarket, we wouldn't get any shares of the next hot IPO.

Time after time, I then took my five thousand shares, bought however much more stock I had to, and simultaneously got rid of it. I would give the brokerage house fifty thousand shares to buy on top of the five they gave us. Meanwhile, I was selling fifty-five thousand with some other brokerage house known for having no investment banking business. This firm is not going to "shut us out" of their next deal, because it doesn't matter to them that we're "flippers." We were in and out with as little actual exposure as possible. The stock I "loved" was gone in a Jim Cramer minute.

Occasionally the issuer distributed shares that could be tracked. The threat was that they would know if you had flipped your allocation. Before I could get too worried, however, the brokers would tell me not to. It was simply too much work. The investment bank took this final precaution for the same reason it created all the others—for the sake of appearances.

"So long as this whole house of cards is still standing," one broker assured me, "we will *never* actually track a deal."

The last thing the brokerage houses did to support this structure was to roll out coverage on these new stocks. The Securities and Exchange Commission made the analysts wait one month before "officially" pushing an IPO. By counting the days from their first trade, we easily determined exactly the date that every brokerage house would then initiate coverage with a rating of strong buy. For a while, Cramer & Company would buy back the stock of an IPO we had initially flipped just before this happened. That worked until it became obvious to everyone on Wall Street that a strong buy rating meant nothing from a brokerage house with an investment banking division. They simply wanted to keep the bubble inflated so more companies could be brought public later.

Maybe I hadn't been completely honest, but the way Jim saw it, we weren't the only ones. It was the brokerage houses that created a facade of legitimacy to manipulate the situation, and ultimately it was the little guy at home, not fully comprehending the process, who bought these stocks at an assuredly inflated value. This, as Jim asserted during that first syndicate briefing, wasn't my concern. Our money had already been made.

Chapter 10

THE NEXT TRAIN DOWNTOWN

A YEAR into my time at Cramer & Company, the same words played over and over in my head like a motivational tape: *This is the opportunity of a lifetime. I am going to make it here, on Wall Street. I am willing to do whatever it takes to succeed.* The longer I submerged myself in this world, the more important this world became.

New York City was definitely growing on me. Beth visited nearly every weekend from New England. We took the subway up to the Bronx and secretly rooted for the Red Sox. We sat outside at a French café in Greenwich Village for Saturday night dinner, and watched the parade of characters walk by. We bought roller blades and joined the masses of people who circle Central Park on summer days. We rode the carousel in the spring and ice-skated in Wollman Rink in the fall.

I hadn't turned on my oven in months. My desk drawer was stuffed with menus from Indian, Thai, Chinese, Italian, Mexican, Japanese, Polish, Turkish, Vietnamese, Cuban, and even typical American restaurants. I could walk two blocks south to Gristede's supermarket, three blocks north for the subway, and right next door for toilet paper. If I needed to get out of the city for a weekend, I took the Delta shuttle back to my parents' country home in Cambridge.

Things were also going exceptionally well at the job. This was, of course, pretty much my life. I was at 56 Beaver Street twelve hours a day every day the stock market was open. I was trading and doing research and a million other things. Scarcely a day went by that I didn't learn something new.

There were certainly some good times early on. Once in a while Jim invoked a team spirit along with his battlefield analogies. He looked around the room and told us all that we would "get through things together." No one was to be trusted except "the few people in this room." On more than one occasion he said almost affectionately, "It's us against the world."

Jim described us as "hogs," which was a good thing. To be a hog meant you were one of the guys on the desk, committed to battling it out every day, putting work above all else. I was proud that I had taken only one day off. Jim had, after all, bet $20 that I could get a construction crew to stop building. He obviously thought I could do a lot. Things like that did foster a sort of camaraderie.

Clark, Mark, and I were going out a few nights a week on our various brokers' expense accounts. We ate at Sparks, Smith and Wollensky's, even Peter Luger's in Brooklyn. If it wasn't steak, we tried Le Cirque, Daniel, or Le Bernardin, all on Smith Barney, Goldman Sachs, or Bear Stearns. After a seven-course meal we threw two hands in the cigar humidor and grabbed as many Monte Cristos as we could. The three of us sat courtside for the Knicks, against the glass for the Rangers, and right behind home plate in Flushing, Queens. We had more best friends than we knew what to do with, all thanks to Jim Cramer's deep-pocketed trading style.

Even Sal mysteriously made a nice gesture one afternoon, giving me a set of golf clubs. He invited me over to his apartment and pulled a bag of Calloways from his closet. Surprised, I told him they were too expensive. "Not to worry," he said as he patted me on the back and pushed me out the door. A week later I confided to Mark how strange the event had seemed, and I learned the whole story. Mark had given the clubs to Sal a year before, and Sal had finally got around to buying himself some new ones. He didn't have enough room in his small apartment for two sets, and that's where I came in.

Marty Peretz was in New York nearly every week those days, and visited the Cramer & Company office all the time. Whenever he saw me, he gave me one of his patented warm hugs, and now and then I even caught Jim looking on approvingly. As I walked him out, Marty told me the great things Jim had said about me.

"Jim says you're doing a terrific job!" He pinched my cheek and smiled.

I told Marty a lot of great things about Jim.

Bonus time came after New Year's, when the accountants finished punching the numbers. We knew what our performance had been as of the close on December 31, but Jim wanted everything finalized. He needed to know exactly what his cut was before he shared the wealth. So each day of January, as the bookkeepers sorted through thousands upon thousands of pages of statements, we came in at 6:30 A.M., hoping that *this* would be the day.

In mid-January, Jim took over Jeff's office for the ceremonies. They met behind closed doors while the rest of us sat at the trading desk. Everyone was trying to look busy and earn those last few brownie points before the big moment. Mark checked some stocks in the Instinet. Sal flipped through the position sheets. Clark and I made sure all the trades from the previous day had been accounted for and everything priced accurately. But despite how all of us tried to pretend otherwise, there was only one thing on each of our minds—money.

Nineteen ninety-four had not been a great year in the market. The Dow Jones closed up only 2 percent while the S&P was down 2 percent. Cramer & Company, going into November with a 6 percent return, gave it all back. Only a decent December helped the fund match the Dow.

Sitting in my seat, looking as busy as I could, I hoped for $5,000.

I reminded myself that my initial commitment to Jim and to myself had not been about money. I *was* excited about what I was learning and doing. I loved the action, throwing millions of dollars around like it was nothing. I loved my new responsibilities. Most of all, I was caught up in the excitement of working for Jim Cramer.

At first I believed in Jim because Marty did. Having been in New York City for a full year, I now recognized how many other people believed in Jim. Everyone in the business knew him. People *not* in the business knew him. He was on television all the time, and barely a week went by that he didn't write an article or have one written about him. And here I was, in January of 1995, having just finished my first year working at *his* company. I knew that even if this didn't pay off today, with the way things were going, it would pay off soon enough.

Actually, I was excited as you could be. Sitting at the trading desk, waiting for Jeff to emerge so I could try to read his expression for any glimmer of excitement or disappointment, I *was* proud of my accomplishments. I had not only survived, but also done pretty well.

"There's only one way to score," Jim always said. "Take the ball and run with it."

I felt I had done exactly that.

As my ass hit the seat cushion in Jeff's office, Jim raced through a few boilerplate pleasantries, like "Good job this year" and "You fought hard." He even produced a smile as he gave me a raise on my base to $30,000, and $15,000 extra to put into my checking account. I'd never seen $15,000 except on television, and I hadn't even been considering a raise. I walked back to the trading desk, telling Clark it was his turn, with a shit-eating grin painted across my face.

The only real problem at this point was that no matter how hard I tried, I never completely forgot that fever I had felt as Jim announced on Day One that we were at war. It came back each and every day as we drove farther into enemy territory, complete with a pit in my stomach and an angst that I just couldn't shake. I was still waking up long before my alarm went off, my forehead damp with sweat, except now I barely slept at all during the night. Sudden spells of dizziness added to the afflictions.

One morning, heading to work at 6:30, I passed out on the Number 4 Express train. The whole experience seemed like a dream. I felt strange and weak, my vision went white, and the next thing I knew I woke up on the floor. The faces of strangers hovered over me, and I had no idea where I was. I remember more than enough people helping me off the train. The quickest way to get the millions of commuters moving again was through just such a strategy.

Sitting by myself on the platform at Fourteenth Street with my head in my hands, I wondered what to do. All the emotions I had been repressing welled up at once. I found myself absolutely terrified to get up, to continue onward to Wall Street station and the Cramer & Company office. There were *so many* reasons to turn around and go home, to hide in my small apartment, not the least of which was a perfectly good medical excuse.

I recognized that I was treading on dangerous ground. Such feelings only stood in my way.

This is the opportunity of a lifetime. I am going to make it here, on Wall Street. I am willing to do whatever it takes to succeed.

I stood up, dusted myself off, and was on the next train downtown.

Chapter 11

"MY FANS WOULD BE LOST WITHOUT ME"

THE ONLY THING Jim loves more than playing the market is talking about the market. Whether it was through television or articles in a host of magazines, he was as enthusiastic about publicity as he was about trading. In 1995 this love would come back to bite him.

Since early 1994 Jim had been writing a column for *Smart-Money* called "Unconventional Wisdom." This was one of the first places Jim could pontificate about the market on a regular basis, and he covered a range of related topics and occasionally made stock picks.

"Pity the Poor Orphans" appeared in the February 1995 edition of *SmartMoney*. The column began, "Often the only difference between a stock that rallies and a stock that languishes is sponsorship. Most stocks, even great ones, need to be pushed before they can rally out of a slump." The subject was "four little orphans we love and why we love them." They were Canonie Environmental, Hogan Systems, Rexon, and UFP Technologies.

Jim made some pretty strong statements about the stocks and offered all kinds of other musings designed to sell the reader, predicting, for example, that "when the move comes, Canonie . . . might triple in price" and that UFPT would "grow like wildfire."

The one thing Jim neglected to mention was that he not only liked these orphans, but had already adopted them. Cramer & Company owned huge slugs of each.

Until then Jim hadn't exhibited significant influence over the market or individual stocks. That's not to say he didn't like to think he did.

"Buy me fifty thousand shares of IBM! Cause an imbalance!" Jim would scream out at the opening. Jim pictured himself as such a "big swinging dick" (he loved to call himself this after his friend Michael Lewis made the term famous in his book *Liar's Poker)* that his trades pushed stocks around. An imbalance resulted if an order was placed so large that the other side couldn't be found, occasionally causing a stock to be halted on the NYSE. Buying fifty thousand shares of IBM, a stock that changes hands millions of times a day, will *not* cause an imbalance. Still, for some reason Jim constantly did this.

"Take fifty thousand shares of America Online! Cause an imbalance!"

In any case, Jim's orphans article actually did have a marked influence. The four stocks were all cheap, trading from $2 to $5 a share, and very illiquid. "Illiquid" means that a stock doesn't trade many shares in a day. If a stock is illiquid, it is more subject to large price swings, because one or two buyers can have a real effect. When the article hit the stands, all the orphans jumped, one making as much as a 100 percent move.

"It's about time the rest of the world woke up to the fact that I'm a fucking genius!" Jim crowed, ecstatic that people were listening to him. When the orphans found a home in other people's accounts just because he pushed them, it was a real ego boost for him.

Jim was even more excited because the fund made a fortune as soon as the article hit the stands. These four stocks were some of the firm's largest positions. In fact, after he wrote the article but before it was published, we had purchased a lot more. The next day, our portfolio valuation showed a huge gain. Jim and Jeff were at the trading desk, laughing and saying that Jim should have written the article sooner. There were a few other holdings in the portfolio that needed to be pushed. And Jim, they agreed, was just the guy to do it.

Truthfully, none of the orphans had been winners for the firm until then. Jim's typical approach was to constantly trade in and out of the market. When he started picking away at these names, he had no intention of ever owning 10 percent of Canonie, Hogan, Rexon, or UFP Technologies. Because they performed so poorly, we continually averaged down, and eventually acquired more shares than we ever imagined we would. Once that happened, because of their illiquid status, it became impossible to sell even had we wanted to. If these stocks were winners from the start, they never would have become core holdings for Cramer & Company. Jim came to love these orphans only by default.

There were plenty of days before Jim wrote the article, and even more after, that he criticized these stocks as perennial "pieces of shit" and "worthless losers."

"We're stuck-holders," Mark put it, "*not* stock-holders."

Jim's euphoria over his article was short-lived. The media frenzy that descended on him and our firm was swift and intense. After the *Washington Post* broke the story, I came into the office to find Jim and Jeff in a closed-door meeting, an ominous sign. After all, Jim spoke to his shrink, talked about jock itch, and fought with his wife from the trading desk.

The *Post* asserted that Jim Cramer had touted stocks he owned, using his influence as a journalist to benefit his personal wealth. Before the ink dried everyone else jumped on board. First was Dan Dorfman on CNBC. Jim and Dan had a running feud in which Jim insulted Dan's actions and motives when he stepped in front of the camera. After the orphans article, Dan got on television and launched into a long tirade that concluded Jim Cramer should go to jail. A host of other papers ran the story, among them the *Wall Street Journal.*

In Jim's defense, *SmartMoney* had neglected to run a disclaimer stating that he might own any of the specific stocks written about. This omission was both one of the reasons the media jumped all over Jim and also why Jim asserted publicly that he was not at fault. No sooner did he blame *SmartMoney* than he admitted to us at the desk that the point was immaterial, anyway. "Like anyone ever put down a pack of cigarettes because of a warning on the side." However a disclaimer might have changed things, Jim found himself at the center of a debate on whether money managers should offer the public stock suggestions.

Journalists, whose primary job is to write, usually don't own a stock they talk about. They have certain insider knowledge of what will be released, and ethical standards dictate that they not misuse such information. If *Business Week* reporters are going to divulge some incremental news on a company or make an opinionated statement, it doesn't look good if they position themselves financially beforehand. This may be why the journalists attacked Jim as ferociously as they did. From their perspective, it wasn't the right thing to do.

Jim was, however, first and foremost a money manager. The money manager's primary job is to pick stocks. This is why most people want to read what money managers write. That their money is riding on a pick adds weight to their claims. Otherwise, we wouldn't care as much about what they had to say. A reporter is a reporter. Jim Cramer is a very successful money manager. Who are you going to pay attention to when it comes to investing?

Whether or not we want to listen to what such people have to say, the system is ripe for abuse. One afternoon on CNBC there was an interview with a well-known portfolio manager. Jim and the rest of us on the trading desk watched as he pushed a stock fervently. After punching at a few keys on his Bloomberg, Jim ascertained that as of the end of the previous quarter, the stock was the largest holding in the billion-dollar fund run by the money manager.

"These fucking people are so predictable," Jim lamented. "If you want to know why anybody's ever saying or doing anything on Wall Street, just ask yourself, 'what's in it for them?'"

In the same way the public loves to hear these opinions, and to a large degree because of it, the process will be manipulated. The truth is, many money managers who write about a stock they like or go on television and say "buy, buy, buy" have already bought themselves.

No one wants to talk others into buying the same stock at the same time they intend to start a position. If there are more buyers than sellers, the stock price becomes inflated, ultimately costing more to acquire shares. On the other hand, creating buyers *after* they've established their own position can make portfolio managers as ecstatic as Jim was when the "orphans" article gave him a quick boost.

Keep in mind these portfolio managers are *not* going to call you up and admit when they start selling. It's more likely that they will still be publicly recommending a position. If they find out that fundamentals have gone south, they will never appear on television again and say there is new, negative information. It's a lot easier to get out when others are still trying to get in. After they've unloaded the position, you won't hear about it again. Jim never mentioned any of the orphans ever again.

This is why so many money managers love to talk about stocks they already own and not about stocks that are sold. They gain nothing by telling about liquidated positions. If they can get you on board after they own it, you might take it that much closer to an exit target. Talking about sales might make someone look good, but that's about it. Next quarter, when they're on television again and the reporter points out, "You picked a loser," the reply will come, "I sold it."

Consider what we told CNBC reporters who called trying to figure out what was happening in a given stock during the day. Our answer was always directly related to our own position. If we owned the stock, we would tell them the buzz was positive and the stock should keep going up. When they passed that on, it gave us the chance to sell. If we were short the stock, we would tell them the buzz was negative and the stock should keep going down. When they passed that on, it gave us the chance to buy the stock back for less. Only if we didn't have a position would we give an unbiased, truthful answer.

With the orphans case, Jim found himself at the center of a firestorm, and he was miserable. He assembled us around the trading desk and announced that the whole world was out to get him. For once, he may have been right. By this point, the SEC had also begun an investigation.

We all stayed until midnight every night that week, sorting through our records to document exactly when we had traded any of the mentioned names. We did it not only for that article, but for all his articles. It took awhile before the furor died down, and the SEC eventually found that Jim had done nothing wrong. Their focus was on whether Jim sold any of the orphans into the spike, and he hadn't.

Waving the SEC document in the air after we were officially vindicated, the former reporter proclaimed, "I'm going to set everyone straight on exactly why business journalists *fucking suck!*

Business journalists cover an industry they *think* they know a lot about, a business that makes those *with balls* incredibly wealthy. These *assholes* are sure they know as much as the next guy about what they *only* write on, but they have no *kahones,* and make like *thirty* grand a year. That makes them all *bitter idiots,* and none of us should *ever* help one, even if they are drowning in their own shit."

Jim looked around the desk to make sure each of us was straight on this point.

"Don't ever forget this! If any one of you *ever* helps these *mother fuckers,* so help me god—" He slammed his hands down on the trading desk.

"If these reporters hadn't stuck their noses where they didn't belong," our commander concluded, "we could have been rid of these shit positions at their *highs.*"

What Jim meant was that the SEC never would have become involved if these other parties hadn't brought the issue to their attention. He always carried on about how inept the SEC was and that they relied on "rats" to figure anything out. The controversy and the attention it brought to the firm made it impossible for us to sell our orphans into the bounce.

Just because we were "stuck-holders" didn't mean a little manipulation couldn't improve the situation, however. Despite the SEC finding that Jim officially did nothing wrong because he hadn't sold any of the orphans, Cramer & Company could still profit off Jim's article. A hedge fund, after all, is structured to pay its managers off of performance, realized *or* unrealized. This means we never had to sell any of the stocks for Jim to benefit personally from the spike. If the orphans were up at the end of the year, we took our 20 percent. It just wouldn't be out of proceeds raised from liquidating those particular names.

Think about what we did on the last trading day of every year. Jim handed Mark a list of illiquid stocks that we owned a huge chunk of, including all the orphans. These stocks were usually dogs we had averaged down in and now owned some unforeseen large amount of. Just before the close of the market, Mark would get to work to make sure all of them were higher at the end of the day. It might take repeated orders or possibly only the purchase of a hundred shares exactly as the bell rang.

Say we owned a million shares of a given stock on the list. If it closed up a point, that was another $1 million to subtract our 20 percent of. Take a yellow legal pad with twenty names on it, and the total adds up. This type of "marking up," as it's called in the industry, might not lead to any long-term appreciation, but we didn't care what happened after December 31. Our management fee was already taken. This practice demonstrates how we could ring the register through *buying* stocks.

At that time, in fact, Cramer & Company was marking the portfolio *twice* a year. A large European concern, Global Asset Management, had given Jim close to $50 million to manage, and he placed their money in an independent account whose year ended on June 30. We were structured to receive performance bonuses in January *and* July. That was before Jim got sick of their "constant hounding" and, after he told them as much, GAM asked for their money back. During this "notice period," Jim took the opportunity to review all the trades at the end of each day and stick a significant amount of losers into their account.

Despite all the attention and debate over the orphans, Jim never took a minute off from trading during the fiasco, and soon found another home for his writing. Regardless of his dislike for business journalists, he wasn't to be dissuaded from talking publicly.

"My fans," he explained on more than one occasion, "would be lost without me."

A few months later, Dan Dorfman himself became the subject of an SEC investigation. Apparently he had been in cahoots with some broker who gave him a few of his ideas, with both men profiting from his hyping stocks. Anyway, Dan had a stroke at some point during all this. He didn't die, but he was off the air.

It was a beautiful summer day when Jim heard about Dan's misfortune. We were all sitting at the trading desk with the window shades pulled down and the air conditioner running full blast. When CNBC reported the news, Jim jumped up from his seat and stood with his face two inches from the screen.

"What a fucking asshole," Jim said. "That's a good way to get out of an SEC investigation. I should have tried that."

Chapter 12

"GANGSTA'S PARADISE"

WAGNER'S *RIDE OF THE VALKYRIES* launched our days in 1995. Just before the opening bell sounded, Jim would turn on a CD player next to his workspace and crank up the volume. He stood there, one foot up on his chair and an arm extended forward like a general about to charge. He screamed orders to "buy" and "sell" as loud as he could over the music.

"I love the smell of money in the morning!"

Once a brokerage house came to us "shopping a print," or trying to arrange a large trade. They had a million shares of a stock to go, and rather than try to work it out slowly, they attempted to get a group of buyers together and put the trade on "in the hole," or at a slight discount from the last sale. Whenever a "size print" like this went up, it was a risky proposition. For one thing, you never knew if the seller was done. Then again, why were they in such a rush to get out?

In any case, Jim bought fifty thousand shares of this print, so-called because the trade is printed on the ticker tape. It looked as if it was going to work for the first few minutes, and Jim prepared to offer the stock he'd just bought for sale.

Then a second brokerage house called and informed us that there would be *another* print of the same stock going on the tape half a point lower than the previous one. We were instantly down $25,000 and had no idea if there was even more stock for sale where that came from. A big seller was apparently jumping from broker to broker, working out of millions (plural) of shares. Essentially they stiffed everyone who bought on the original print.

Jim called the trader at the first brokerage house.

"You just fucked me up the ass without a drop of KY jelly."

He added that he wanted to "DK" (don't know) the trade, which was back office jargon for when a stock mistakenly ends up in someone's account and you reject delivery.

The trader apologized and assured Jim that he had no idea the seller was about to reload with another million. Jim turned crimson and the veins in his forehead bulged.

"I'm going to pull the fucking wire right *now,* if you don't take back the trade."

I have no idea what else the guy said, but it obviously didn't work. Jim smashed the phone down on his desk before ripping the cord out of the phone turret and throwing the receiver across the room. It dented the wall and slid to the floor.

"Pulling a wire" was a symbol of disconnecting a relationship with a broker. Of course, what Jim actually did was yank his only phone cord out of the extension. The line to the broker was still there. Only now Jim couldn't call *any*one. This only made him angrier.

"Somebody better give me a new fucking phone, *right fucking now!!!*"

The next day, in an unrelated incident except for the outcome, Jim asked Mark to buy ten thousand shares of Intel. It was a simple, run-of-the-mill trade. The type of order Jim gave Mark hundreds of times a day, and Mark executed over and over. Mark checked his Level Two Nasdaq screen and the Instinet, and elected to call a Salomon Brothers market maker who was on the offer side, apparently trying to sell. At the time Jim gave the order, the futures were ticking up and buyers were coming into the market.

The trader at Salomon Brothers sold us our ten thousand Intel, and no sooner did we receive a report than the stock began to plunge. Mark started to tell Jim that we bought ten thousand shares of Intel at three-quarters, but before he could finish his sentence it was offered at five-eighths, then a half. Obviously, someone had a huge seller.

"That fucking guy plugged us!" Jim yelled at Mark. "He fucking plugged us!"

"We don't know that," Mark replied.

"Whose fucking side are you on?" Jim leaned over his terminals and shook a fist at Mark.

"Lehman, Goldman, Smith Barney—they all came in with the stock to go, also," Mark continued.

"Do I have to handle everything? Am I the only one who will fight for this fucking firm?" Jim screamed. Nobody spoke. Mark seemed to recognize that it might have been better if he had kept his mouth shut.

"Jim," Mark tried to calm him down.

"Am I the only one here who will fight for this firm?" Jim shrieked. He started romping around behind his workstation, flailing his arms in the air.

"I said, *am I the only one here who will fight for this firm?*"

His beady brown eyes glared at each of us. Mark looked at Jim without saying anything. Sal was making the same scowling face. Clark kept his head down and punched numbers into a calculator. I slid down in my seat, trying to hide behind a monitor. Jeff was in his office.

"Bunch of *fucking cowards!*" Jim screamed as he picked up his new receiver and hit the Salomon Brothers wire. Before the trader could say a thing, Jim yelled, "I'm coming over there to kick your ugly fucking ass all the way back to Long Island, *mother fucker!*"

He turned and sprinted out the front door of our office.

The room was dead silent. We all looked at each other.

Jeff came out of his office. "Where'd Jim go?"

"He went—" Mark stopped short.

"He went?" Jeff wanted an answer.

"He went to go kick someone's ugly fucking ass all the way back to Long Island," Mark said.

"What?"

"I said, he went to kick someone's ugly fucking ass all the way back to Long Island."

"Oh." Jeff turned and went back into his office.

"I don't think that guy even lives in Long Island," Mark muttered.

Ten minutes later Jim reappeared, still fuming.

"The only thing that saved that mother fucker was security at World Trade Center," Jim explained. "They wouldn't let me up. Otherwise, that guy would have learned firsthand that *nobody* rips off Jim Cramer and gets away with it!"

Later that week, a person made the mistake of giving us someone else's allotment of a hot IPO. There was another hedge fund on the Street called Cramer Rosenthal, and people were always confusing us (this rarely happened a second time). An assistant called and told us we had a great allocation, far more than we were expecting or usually received.

"You're giving me *twenty thousand* shares?" I was on the trading desk when he told me this, and I spoke loudly so Jim could hear. The guy confirmed it. I asked again, "You're *sure* that's right? *Twenty thousand?*"

The guy confirmed it once more.

We all high-fived each other, because the IPO was indicated to open up twenty points. Just then the broker called me back. His assistant had made a mistake. Our allocation was only *two* thousand shares. The assistant gave us Cramer Rosenthal's allocation by accident.

"*Now* you're telling me that my allocation is just two thousand shares?" I asked.

As soon as Jim heard me, he bit down on his bottom lip so hard I thought he might just swallow half of his face.

"That assistant confirmed it not *once,* but *twice!*" Jim shouted before the broker could say anything else. "This is *their* fucking problem, now. Hang up on that fucking liar, right now!"

I hung up.

Two seconds later my line rang.

"Don't answer it!" Jim yelled.

I didn't.

My line went silent and Jim's immediately started to ring. He sat in his seat and stared stonily at his monitors.

"*No one* is to pick up the *mother fucking* phone," Jim instructed.

In a matter of minutes, numerous lines were ringing. We all simply tried to ignore them, which was hard, considering the pressure we were usually under to answer them. Mark leaned forward at one point, the first to break.

"Mark!" Jim snapped. "*What did I say?*"

Mark sat back, empty-handed.

Finally Jim realized that he was eventually going to have to talk to someone outside of the office. He called the broker and told him, "It's too late. I already sold the twenty thousand shares."

I looked at my monitor to see that this was impossible, since the IPO hadn't even opened for trading.

Jim didn't leave the broker time to point this out. "If you want to be a fucking Indian giver faggot," he said, "then you should be fucking embarrassed for yourself, being such a lowlife scumbucket."

Those who found themselves on Jim's bad side could expect to be there for some time. Jim was capable of holding grudges like no one else I have ever met. To say Jim held a grudge does not, in fact, do him justice. That Clark couldn't be called by his real name, Larry, only begins to tell the story.

One of the many people at the top of Jim's hate list was Seth Tobias, a fairly well known money manager who got his start working for Jim. Seth went on to run a hedge fund called Circle T Partners and often appeared on CNBC. Seth's unforgivable sin had been to leave Jim's little world of his own volition.

"I taught that guy everything I knew, then he just got up and left for more money! Greedy little shit." Jim shook his head with disappointment at the memory. Seth "Ass Hole" Tobias, as Jim called him, could not be mentioned without derogatory adjectives added in as if they were part of his name.

"Seth 'Traitor' Tobias" was Sal's variation. Every time Seth was on television, Sal would say, "There he goes, making shit up, *again.*"

Jeff chimed in about how wrong Seth was, no matter what he said, and the rest of us emphatically agreed. Jim listened approvingly from behind his monitors to our criticisms until he would finally turn the channel.

"I can't listen to such a fucking moron anymore."

There was another trader who had worked for Jim and Karen before I arrived. For *years* after he left, even if there was no reason to, Jim found occasion to ridicule him. He didn't appear on television, like Seth. Still, out of the blue, Jim would think to lay into the guy. I never met him, but I felt as if I knew Michael. He was a spineless coward who couldn't do anything right. The rest of us would laugh and say, "What a loser."

The change from friend to foe could come at any time. When Jim first went on CNBC, he came back as excited as a child on Christmas morning about having hung out with celebrities. The reporters on CNBC were regulars on every trading desk up and down Wall Street.

"I'm friends with all of them," Jim explained.

He talked about how close he was to Maria Bartiromo, in particular.

"She won't leave me alone," he added.

Maria did call and ask to speak with him on a few occasions. More often, Jim called her. He was delighted to have Maria's direct number, and he used it often. While appearing on CNBC, he made it a daily routine to try and help members of the television crew by alerting them to any developing story or the upgrades and downgrades various analysts made. We were the first firm most brokerage houses told such news, and Jim decided to use this early-call status to help the reporters, who all wanted to break a story.

Jim's strategy was to put in his order to buy a stock with Mark and then dial Maria. As soon as she announced the news on television, the stock would often jump. Jim then had Mark peel off whatever we had bought.

Jim was, essentially, both helping and using Maria. He'd give her the scoop, and before things settled down, she spread the news that was likely to get the stock running. We weren't just using the news, but making it. No sooner would Maria be thanking us for the help than we'd be getting a payback—a quick hit thanks to our friend at CNBC.

This went on for a while, until one morning I answered a call from Maria, who wanted to speak with Jim.

"I'm never talking to Maria again!" Jim announced when I told him she was on the phone. "I've gone out of my way to help her one too many times. *Understand?*"

I nodded.

"*Fuck that bitch!*" Jim slammed a hand down on the trading desk.

Jeff later explained that Jim felt Maria had slighted him at a party the previous evening. She was talking to a group of people and Jim pushed himself into their conversation. Apparently, Maria didn't drop everything to welcome him.

"She probably just wasn't enthusiastic enough to see him," was how Jeff put it.

Whatever happened, Cramer & Company never helped Maria Bartiromo again. It was David Faber we were now instructed to call with any early tips after buying the stock. Things ended up working out quite well, as David soon proved to be an even more profitable friend to have.

One slow Friday in early November 1996, our latest secretary told Jim that David was on the phone, asking for him. Jim answered the line, and in a moment his eyes went wide and he sprang out of his seat. He hung up the receiver, leaned over his monitors, and insisted that Mark buy a hundred thousand shares of MCI.

"Just take it! Get it in!!!"

Mark picked up the Goldman Sachs trading wire and placed the order with our broker, Bernadette.

"I need a hundred thousand shares of MCI, *now!*" Mark said, adding, "There *will* be news!"

Mark knew that if Goldman sold us the stock short they would scream bloody murder if news came out five seconds later. The way Jim was pulling his hair out waiting for a report indicated to Mark that he knew *something* good was about to materialize. A moment later, Bernadette called back and told our head trader that we had bought our hundred thousand shares of MCI.

It couldn't have been more than an hour before David appeared on CNBC reporting a breaking story. MCI was in play. This meant that someone was looking to acquire the company. David added that he heard this from a reliable source and the deal would be done at a significant premium to the current share price. No sooner had he opened his mouth than buyers started rushing in to take the stock. MCI jumped upwards violently as viewers frantically tried to capitalize on the story that most were just now hearing for the first time.

Jim was laughing and spinning around in his chair when the Goldman trading wire rang. It was Bernadette. She thanked Mark for the tip. Goldman Sachs not only bought us our hundred, but bought themselves a like amount, yielding a big hit to their own P & L.

"I owe you one," Bernadette added.

"On Wall Street," Mark explained, "information is coin."

After the close, MCI and British Telecom confirmed the news. BT, a 10 percent holder of MCI, was now interested in buying the rest of the company it did not yet own. Although it would eventually be WorldCom that won MCI, our money was already in the register.

Only David and Jim will ever know what was actually said during that brief call. I'll be the first to admit that reporters often called us, asking if we could confirm a rumor in the marketplace. We were, after all, a "good source." All I can say is that in this instance, for once Jim only listened instead of speaking.

During my time at Cramer & Company, barely a day went by without some kind of rumor getting around. It could be that the Federal Reserve chairman was retiring, that some CEO had died, or that a specific company was about to release important news. It might have some basis in reality, even if just speculation on a hastily called conference call, or it could come from nowhere. I've seen Intel, Sun Micro, IBM, and many others go flying up or down in a matter of minutes on a juicy rumor.

The very nature of rumors makes them ripe for abuse. Financial markets work to be ahead of the curve. Everyone is always struggling to find out what news might come next. This makes speculation commonplace. Jim knew firsthand that it was all too easy to perpetuate the rumor mill for a big hit.

Jim would often hear news of some kind, establish a position, and then have us spread the rumor. If we found out something that might be important, Jim didn't want it to get around until we were ready to capitalize. Whether the news was true or not had nothing to do with it. All that mattered was whether other traders might believe it was true. A good story, regardless of whether it's ultimately correct, can move a stock in the interim.

In addition to his CNBC connections, he was personally calling our brokers and other fund managers, spreading whatever had been heard. Most rumors are bullshit, as he knew, but so long as you're not the last one to buy it or overstay your welcome, money can be made. If the stock jumped, he would happily sell his shares to any one of those original people he had called.

There was one time in particular when we were getting hit pretty badly in a position and things, as they often could, were getting ugly. Jim had averaged down in Motorola, which didn't appear to be bouncing at all. It was beginning to cost us dearly.

Jim was out of his mind, pacing back and forth behind his desk, constantly watching his monitors. He looked as if he hadn't slept in days. His brown eyes seemed to pop from his skull, and he pulled at his tie, trying to suck in more air. Suddenly he leaned over his computers toward Mark. "I heard that Motorola is about to land a major contract. Get it out there!"

The reason we were in the stock was that another speculator

had told us that morning that "some kind of good news will be coming out in Motorola." When we heard that, Jim bought in. The rumor hadn't materialized yet, so Jim decided to facilitate things by adding a few details to the story. He felt that it was merely further speculation on the original speculation. Of course, the folks we spread the updated rumor to were not given this disclaimer.

One of the lowest things I ever saw Jim do was threaten someone's children. Jim ordered Mark to buy ten thousand shares of Pfizer. Usually when Jim gave orders he qualified them. He might say, "Just bid for it." This meant he wasn't in a rush, and we would try to work it in at a slight discount. Or he might say, "Buy half and bid for half." This was more of a middle ground. Get some in at any price, and then try to acquire some lower. Another alternative was, "Take it." Buy the stock at market price.

With the Pfizer order, Jim told Mark to take it. Mark gave the order to a broker exactly as it was given to him, and we waited for our report. Whenever you place a "market order" there are risks. Jim saw ten thousand shares of Pfizer for sale at fifty. So he put in an order to buy ten thousand shares at "the market," assuming he would be taking the stock offered at fifty. Unfortunately, someone else had put in *another* market order to buy ten thousand shares a few seconds before we did. They took the shares at fifty, and suddenly we saw *our* ten thousand go on the tape at fifty and a half.

Jim, as he always did, was watching *every* trade of Pfizer. He'd seen ten thousand shares go on the tape at fifty a second after he placed his order, and he instantly knew that someone else beat him to the offered stock. It can take a minute or two for your order to get to the floor of the NYSE through a broker. By the time Mark was receiving Jim's report, the stock had traded back down to fifty.

"*This is unacceptable!*" Jim screamed before Mark could even confirm the news.

The broker recognized this was a bad report, especially considering that the stock now traded lower. He knew we lost $5,000 on the print. Yet he rightfully argued that it was given to him as a market order. Mark relayed the broker's case to Jim.

With one swipe of his arm, Jim cleared stacks of paperwork, a laptop, and his steamed vegetables from Hanover off his desk and onto the floor.

"*This is unacceptable!*" he repeated through gritted teeth.

Hearing the broker still argue, Jim pointed at the phone in Mark's hand and exclaimed, "He's taking food from my children's mouths!"

He jumped onto the desk and tried climbing over his monitors to reach Mark's phone. He grabbed the receiver from Mark's hand.

"*Where the fuck is your family? Where the fuck is your family?*" he screamed. "You think you can take food from my kids' mouths? You think you can steal from *my children?*"

Mark and the rest of us around the desk stepped back a few feet because it looked as if Jim might charge at any of us. He continued to yell into the receiver.

"Where do your kids go to school? Where do your kids go to school? I'm going to be there when they get out, mother fucker!!!"

He smashed the phone to pieces, ending the call, and then faced us all to repeat his familiar mantra.

"This is Wall Street! This is what we do!"

Jim's approach to trading was ruthless. He felt that all's fair in times of war, and if things didn't go his way, he would *never* sit and take it. Nor did he ever discuss something calmly. He would scream, yell, jump around, and break things while threatening the wrath of God upon whomever he thought deserved it. It was his style, and we all had to accept it.

Plain and simple, the reason *why* Jim acted in this manner was that such tactics often worked. Calling someone "a faggot Indian giver" got him an extra few thousand shares of a red-hot IPO. Elaborating on a Motorola rumor that had lost its fizzle got him out of a losing position. By threatening someone's children, he eventually got an "adjusted" price and saved a considerable amount of money. *Everyone* was expendable, since there was always someone else willing to give him what he wanted. Just look at what came of Jim's fight with Maria Bartiromo.

Over the years the style of attack never changed, only the music that drove us ever forward. After *Ride of the Valkyries* came other inspirational anthems, until one rap song, "Gangsta's Paradise," stayed on the top of Jim's chart.

Power in the money, money in the power, minute after minute, hour after hour . . .

Jim stood behind his monitors, head bobbing like a pigeon's to the beat. His fingers randomly curled in what he believed to be gang hand signals as he sang along with Coolio in his high-pitched whine. Every so often he pointed an imaginary gun toward any one of us and pulled the trigger.

Been spending most our lives, living in a gangsta's paradise. Keep spending most our lives, living in a gangsta's paradise.

Chapter 13

"DON'T COME BACK, MOM"

MY MOMENTUM slowed in mid-1995. The anxiety, which earlier manifested as a gnawing annoyance in the back of my head, was now becoming a prevalent sense of panic. This feeling inevitably hit any time I came within a block of the office. My stomach was in constant knots, and I didn't have the appetite for anything on the Hanover Deli menu. Nearly every moment I thought that I *must* be forgetting to worry about *something*.

Still, I kept pushing these feelings back. I tried to summon my original fervor, returning to the commitment I had made to give this job everything, 110 percent. I viewed my irrepressible feelings as weakness and was *not* going to allow them to prevent me from thriving. I *am* tough enough to make it here, I told myself. *Nothing will keep me down.*

Regardless of what I tried to tell myself, the daily beatings continued. If Jim was screaming at a broker, eventually he had to hang up the phone. The five of us were with him all day. We each took our inevitable turns in the doghouse.

Mark, with no concern for proper etiquette, continued to try to be fair and friendly. Jim was constantly furious with him for defending the brokers who were *always* taking us for an eighth of a dollar. I watched Jim cringe every time his head trader said "please" and "thank you" on the phone. Mark's niceties often sent Jim fleeing from the trading desk to Jeff's office. From behind the closed door came words like "buffoon" and "moron."

Clark, still attempting to keep his head down, would inevitably be called on to provide an average price or a total number of shares. Although Jim had an uncanny ability to keep track of all the thousands of trades he made, now and then he would ask for confirmation. Clark would lift his head from the endless back office work only long enough to give what was directly required of him. If he happened to be off by a few cents on an average or by a few thousand shares on a position, the shit hit the fan.

Even Sal spent time in the doghouse. *His* day there started like any other, with typical attempts to make "friends." First he told Mark that he had the sense of humor of a "circus clown." Then he turned to Clark, who neglected to staple one page of the position sheets into his copy, and asked him if he had been "dropped on his head as a child." (I was fortunate enough to be completely ignored by him up to this point.)

Then Sal sold five hundred IBM calls when Jim asked him to buy five hundred.

"If you weren't so busy sticking your tongue up my ass," Jim snapped, "maybe you could get kindergarten shit right!"

I don't think the rest of us could have asked for a better gift. Our pleasures had been reduced to reveling in someone else's misfortunes. If Jim was insulting Sal, at least he wasn't insulting us.

As for me, I was temporarily struck with a feeling of moral obligation to actually *hold on to* an IPO after telling the investment bankers I would do just that. A broker at Alex Brown (since swallowed up by Banker's Trust) talked me into buying the "next FedEx," a small shipping company called Fine Air. No sooner had I bought my fifty thousand shares in the aftermarket, *without* simultaneously selling it somewhere else, than one of their thirteen planes crashed in Miami. Apparently, the Federal Aviation Administration had been investigating Fine Air for some time before the IPO. I don't recall this fact being included in the prospectus. If Alex Brown hadn't rescinded the entire deal, I would have been banished from the trading desk for far longer than my week in the doghouse.

There were months on end when all of us were in the doghouse. If anyone told Jim something he already knew, which was everything, he became enraged.

Let's say some news about a position hit the Dow Jones tape. You tell Jim, "IBM's earnings on the tape." It's better to be safe than sorry, you're thinking. If it's new news, Jim should know about it. But the earnings came out an hour ago and you were in the bathroom. This is unforgivable.

"That news was out five fucking years ago," Jim shouts from behind his monitors.

"Yeah, five fucking years ago!" Sal adds, glaring at you.

Or let's say you see a headline that really is new news. You happen to be watching the Dow Jones tape and catch it right away. You say, "Intel, increasing their buyback, on the tape."

"I can read the fucking tape myself," Jim barks.

"Yeah, we can read the fucking tape," Sal agrees.

Now you decide that maybe it's simply best to keep your mouth shut. There goes a headline on a stock that the company happens to own fifty thousand shares of. But Jim and Sal have already cut you to shreds, and it seems easier not to say anything. The stock starts plummeting right away, and Jim isn't reacting.

"What the fuck is wrong with EMC?" he asks.

You mention there was a headline.

"What *the fuck* is wrong with *you?*" For once, Jim hasn't seen it. "You want us to just *lose* money?"

Before the monitor hits the floor, the echo known as Sal chimes in.

You might think that such an attitude was reserved only for when something went wrong. Jim's approach, though, was full-time attitude. This type of extreme behavior had to be maintained at all times.

After recapping all of our trades with a broker one Friday afternoon, I told him to "have a nice weekend."

"Have a nice weekend?" Jim stood up from behind his terminals and shot me a furious look. "'Have a nice weekend' is for *me* and your *mother. No* one else."

Maybe I could tell my mother to have a nice weekend, but that didn't mean she was welcome at Cramer & Company.

Several times Jim invited my mother to drop by the office. An avid reader of the *New York Times Book Review,* Jim would often greet me on Monday mornings by saying that he had read another review that my mom or dad wrote for the paper.

"When are your parents dropping in?" he'd ask.

"Soon," I replied with more than a little trepidation.

My mother finally agreed to Jim's invitation to come down to Wall Street. How was I supposed to tell Mom that I needed her to call from the pay phone downstairs before she came up? I pictured myself saying, "You have to call from downstairs because that leaves the *least* amount of time possible for things to go wrong between when you hang up the phone and enter the office." The last thing I wanted was for my mother to hear Jim call someone an "ass reaming faggot cocksucker" and then get hit with a flying computer monitor.

Anyway, my mom came into the office *just* as we were, of course, losing money in some position. Jim was pulling the few curls of hair he had left out of his head as I introduced her. He tried to smile, said "hi" because "hello" would have taken too long, and gave me a glare that screamed "Not now!"

"I'd love to chat," Jim announced while turning back to the disaster at hand. "But I'm getting *fucking killed* right now."

Any detached observer might think that Jim's treatment of my mother should have been enough to push me over the edge. Unfortunately, I didn't have the luxury of looking at my situation from a distance. I was in the thick of it, and even though this event ultimately did serve as a catalyst for me, at the time it forced me to accept that there could be no turning back. If I wanted to survive at Cramer & Company and on Wall Street, I'd have to follow my general wherever he led.

"Come on." I grabbed Mom's arm and showed her to the hallway. I placed her on the elevator and, as the doors closed, warned, "Don't come back, Mom."

A few days later our fax machine broke. Every time a fax came in, the handset rang five times incredibly loudly and nonstop. No one knew what was wrong with it. We couldn't turn the ringer off or even lower the volume. It just kept ringing and ringing and ringing.

"Rip the fucking thing out of the wall," Jim finally said to me.

I stood up, walked over to it, and lifted the entire machine into the air. I pulled as hard as I could and ripped it straight out of the wall. It stopped ringing, and we all returned to work.

"Where the fuck is that important fax I'm expecting?" Jim asked half an hour later. Standing next to the fax machine, I tried to reconnect it while Jim went on, "I was expecting *a very fucking important fax. Where is my fucking fax.* You just fucked absolutely *everything* up!"

Before I realized what I was doing, I lifted the fax machine over my head and threw it to the ground. Seeing its circuit boards and wires spread over the floor wasn't enough. I needed that fax machine to *pay.* I jumped on its cracked plastic exterior, spreading its innards across the floor. I kicked that fax machine as hard as I could, and I told it, I told that damn fax machine, "*You stupid fucking fax machine!!!*"

That's when it dawned on me. I was ready to fight back. Some-one must *always* pay. I might not know who, or maybe even why, only that I could be damn sure there would be casualties. Some-one was going to take a bullet, and now I caught on—better you than me. The only way to keep Jim off my back was to get on yours. Standing on top of the destroyed fax machine, I looked over at Jim. He was smiling.

The next day I came into the office to find our Bloomberg down. On occasion, when I'd arrive at 6:30 in the morning, one of our market data services would be out of order, be it Bloom-berg, Bridge, or ILX. It might have been our terminals, but more often it was systemwide. Jim relied on these providers for quotes, news, nearly everything we needed to stay in touch and operate. This is why we subscribed to three or four providers at a time. If one went down, it wouldn't cripple us. Still, Jim was livid when it happened.

"I am going to have you fired from your stupid fucking thirty-thousand-dollar-a-year job by the end of the day if my Bloom-berg isn't running in five minutes!" I heard Jim say, laying into some customer service representative like there was no tomorrow.

When the Bloomberg wasn't fixed within the given time period, Jim called the rep back and demanded to talk with a manager. "I am going to have *you* fired from your stupid fucking thirty-thousand-dollar-a-year job by the end of the day if my Bloomberg isn't running in five minutes!!!" he told the manager.

When that didn't work, the torch was passed to me.

The first time this had happened, a while before, I had screamed at a dial tone for a few minutes. Everyone on the desk had been watching, and I couldn't go easy. Jim and Sal wanted results. I told that dial tone it had no idea of the severity of the situation. I even threw in a few swears and threats. I needed some practice before I would be strong enough to do it for real.

This time, with our service down and destruction of a fax machine under my belt, I called with no intention of screaming at a dial tone. I wanted my own customer service rep, and I wanted him *now!* I stood up from my seat with the receiver to my ear and everyone on the desk watching.

"I am going to have you fired from your stupid fucking thirty-thousand-dollar a year job by the end of the day if my Bloomberg isn't running in five minutes!!!"

When breakfast rolled around an hour later, Hanover sent up two bad fruit cups. Before Jim and Jeff could even complain, I had dialed their number.

"There's *nothing* nastier than *old* melon! It gets squishy. Honeydew *has* to be fresh or it loses *all* its flavor. This tastes like rotten yogurt!"

Later that day, a trader gave me a bad execution on an order. He told me I bought my ten thousand shares at a half when now the shares were offered at a quarter. Before he could explain, *I* explained it to *him*.

"You just fucked me up the ass without a drop of KY jelly."

I had not joined this fray to do anything other than win it all. I was ready to take it to the next level. If we were at war, and if I wanted to live, I needed to learn how to fight. And that's exactly what I did. I acted as my general wanted. I took the offensive and decided to attack before I was attacked.

By the end of the day, I managed to blame everything that went wrong on someone else before it could be blamed on me. I took credit for everything others did right. As I pushed my way onto a crowded uptown train while the conductor tried to close the doors, it hit me. I had gone an entire day without getting screamed at.

Chapter 14

"FEEL THE PAIN"

FROM MY FIRST DAYS at Cramer & Company, I wanted to do it all. I tackled ordering meals and opening mail, then research and trading. Having now been exposed to all elements of the business, I recognized there was one more hill to conquer. I hungered, above all else, to make the big call. I wanted to pick stocks.

Just three months into my time at Cramer & Company I stumbled into my first recommendation. At 10:55 A.M. I was placing lunch orders when Jeff came out of his office and announced there were three conference calls the firm needed to listen to. Jim Cramer could do a lot, but he couldn't listen to three conference calls at the same time. Jeff took one, Jim another, and I was assigned the third.

Ten minutes later, while listening to one call himself, Jim stood up behind his monitors and looked over at me. At Cramer & Company, I learned a whole new language of hand signals and expressions. On a trading desk, there are a number of ways to tell someone next to you one thing while you also have a phone to each ear. In this case, with both hands in the air and a receiver nestled under his chin, Jim was clearly asking, "What do you think of the call?"

At that moment, I had been listening to the CFO of Sears go on about LIFO credits. This was my first conference call, and I thought the guy sounded pretty good (they almost always *sound* good), so I gave the thumbs up sign. Before I realized what happened, Jim instantly pointed to Mark and started bringing his arms frantically toward himself to tell him to buy the stock. Mark asked how much, and Jim held up both hands, so we took ten thousand shares.

I didn't mean that Jim should necessarily *buy* the stock, but it was already too late. As a cold sweat broke out on my forehead, I thought to myself that the call still seemed to be going pretty well, as far as I could tell, except that I had no idea what a LIFO credit was. Toward the end of the call, Sears made some conservative comments.

Later that afternoon Jim and I had a private conversation in the back file room. The action we should have taken was to sell, not buy. The mistake cost us $20,000. Jim was livid.

"I want you to *feel the pain*," Jim explained as the corners of his mouth hung down in a fierce scowl. "Let me make a hundred percent sure you understand what I mean by this." He looked me in the eye. "There is *nothing* as bad as losing money. I wouldn't feel worse if any one of you had died today."

With this introduction, I watched and waited for my next opportunity. I understood the consequences of making a wrong decision, and for some reason that only increased my appetite to find a winner. Despite my initial lesson, I was prepared, even eager, to try again.

My second summer in New York, shortly after I'd made yet another leap forward in my progress at Cramer & Company by kicking my mother out of the office and beating up a fax machine, I received my long-awaited second chance.

My girlfriend, Beth, came to stay with me in between her junior and senior years of college. She was working full-time at a Gap store around the corner from my studio on Thirty-ninth Street. Beth hadn't even been there a few weeks when they started cutting back her hours. I told her that there was a Gap store on every other corner in New York and she should go work at another one. She replied that her manager told her they were cutting back everyone's hours at all the stores. That's how they handled things if sales were down, the manager explained.

At the time, the stock was still enjoying the tail end of a decade of spectacular performance. No one on Wall Street knew that trends may have slowed for the specialty retailer. The Gap said nothing, since it always remains silent on sales trends between official releases. Some companies provide updates at any time. The Gap chose to wait until they released monthly figures, which in this case were only a few days away. "Same-store sales," as they're called in the retail industry, are a measure of whether a company has done better or worse than in the previous year. The idea that I might have stumbled on something significant excited the hell out of me.

I approached Jim as he sat at the trading desk, squeezing a sponge ball with one hand while stabbing the tip of a ballpoint pen into the desk with the other. We had averaged down in a losing position that some broker put us into, and Jim was fuming. Having seen Jeff in action, I knew I would have to present my idea in a sentence or two. Perhaps this wasn't the most ideal time, but I felt even worse saying nothing. If it did go down, I'd kill myself.

"Jim, I'm not sure if this is important, but I think the Gap might not be doing so well. My girlfriend works there, and she said they've cut back on everyone's hours—"

"Mark," Jim instantly blurted out. "Short fifty thousand shares of GPS."

I turned around and walked back to my seat feeling an unmatched rush that inevitably comes the moment money has been laid on the table but the dice have yet to roll.

While I continued to follow every hundred-share lot of the stock that traded (GPS will trade a few million shares, easy, on a normal day) I felt as if my heart was in my throat. When the stock went up a half point (the *wrong* way when you're betting on a decline), Jim told Mark to short *another* fifty thousand shares. I was sliding lower in my seat when Jim stood up and looked right at me.

"How does it feel to have your balls in the frying pan?" he asked. He held up a picture he had drawn to demonstrate his question. The image, in bright red marker, showed two round nuts being heated in a large skillet over a flame.

Two days later, before the opening, all the retailers were reporting their same-store sales. I was a nervous wreck. Beth even claimed that I sat up in the middle of the night and screamed, "Sell! Sell! Sell!" I was in the bathroom puking when Jeff banged on the door and told me the news. GPS saw their first negative sales comparison in six months, considerably lower than expectations. I lifted my head from the toilet and felt a rush of adrenaline that I'm not sure has ever been matched. This was a *big* hit! I walked out of that bathroom and into the trading room on cloud nine.

The stock opened a point and a half lower than it had closed the previous day, and Mark got to work covering our short. When all was said and done, we made over $100,000. Jim gave me a thousand bucks then and there, and another two for "some half-decent suits." That Saturday Jeff took me to Barney's, and my old interview garb was on its way to the Salvation Army. For the first time, Jim told me "good job," and meant it.

The next week, I tried to figure out what to do for an encore. I recognized that Jeff and Jim already had their contacts in the world of technology. They knew about routers and mainframes and storage in ways that I could never understand. There was no point in my trying to cover Silicon Valley. I decided to take my Hannaford Brothers, Sears, and Gap experience and run with that. I would do retail stocks.

I got to work learning the department stores, the discounters, the apparel manufacturers, and even the textile companies. I went on a Goldman Sachs supermarket field trip to Arizona and visited five different bakery sections in a single day. I cruised the malls with Morgan Stanley in Palm Beach, Florida. I saw designer showrooms with Smith Barney and previewed next season's lines. I even learned the difference between a brown shoe and a white shoe.

With the arrival of 1996, I had my own portfolio and a few positions on the sheets. That January, when the firm moved from 56 Beaver Street around the corner to 100 Wall Street, in addition to a spot on the trading desk, I was *even* given an office.

My timing could not have been better to become an enthusiastic retail analyst. The Federal Open Market Committee was lowering interest rates, which is traditionally the time one wants to buy these stocks in the hope that consumer spending will jump-start. Recognizing this, I went long the entire group, even buying GPS with the expectation of a recovery.

Everything went exceptionally well at first. Jim used two of my best ideas as picks in his January 15, 1996, cover story for *New York* magazine, in which he put together a portfolio of ten stocks for the new year. One was Dayton Hudson, a retailer that has since been renamed for its best performing division, Target. They were about to storm into the New York area, which I hoped would show the local portfolio managers firsthand what a better company they were than one of their competitors in the discount space, Kmart. At the other end of the spectrum was the luxury retailer Gucci. With some work, I determined that it wasn't just Jeff loading up on their loafers and other merchandise.

Both stocks became huge hits for the firm and me. By the time Jim took the opportunity to reflect on his picks in mid-1996, Gucci had nearly doubled and Dayton Hudson was up 50 percent. I was thrilled that my work directly contributed to Jim's being able to gloat over the performance of his "New York portfolio." Even better, my individual P & L also posted the majority of Cramer & Company's profits while managing only a fraction of the assets through the second quarter of the year.

By the summer of my third year at the fund, I had made over $14 million for Cramer & Company. Jeff was asking me what I thought of various stocks and the market as a whole. Jim called my home one Friday night to tell me that he had never seen *anyone* trade as well as me. He introduced me to visitors as the Golden Boy and gave me carte blanche to pick stocks. *I* was saying "che-*ching*" and calling the shots, in a *big* way.

I should have known it wouldn't last. I was too busy charging forward to know when to let up. By the end of the summer, the bloom had come off the retail rose. The economic cycle moved on, and new sectors grew in favor. In the fall, I gave back a few of the $14 million I initially made. Yes, I made a *lot* of money. But the way Jim looked at it, I lost a few million. After all, when Jim called me at home that Friday night, he had already factored what was raked in. He now wanted $50 million.

I was too slow to take profits. I tried to hold a few stocks, despite having learned that "hold" was a four-letter word at Cramer & Company. In my defense, I never would have made as much as I did if I flipped everything after the stocks were up an eighth. Nevertheless, Jim was furious. I might have done better succumbing the very first time Jim tried to sell every name in my portfolio for a $50,000 hit. The millions I made were no longer the focus. That I hadn't rung the register soon enough was.

Day after day, Jim ripped me apart. Every mistake became inexcusable. Once a Smith Barney retail analyst with whom I had developed a good relationship confided that a certain company was going to report better than expected monthly sales. We bought a nice slug of stock shortly before they reported numbers as expected, neither better nor worse than estimates. The price dropped half a point, and Jim was furious.

"Nick," he pointed out in front of everyone in the office, "you were played like a fiddle."

After that, Jim stopped talking to me. I could say "good morning" and get no response. It wasn't even simply a cold shoulder. Hearing my voice, seeing my face, caused him great anguish. He wanted nothing to do with me. I sat at the trading desk and was ignored. While I was in the doghouse, none of the other guys on the desk would be nice, either. Sal constantly insulted me for Jim's benefit. Mark and Clark kept their distance. Jeff spoke to me only if Jim was out of the room.

It happened to be *that* October when I was set to marry Beth. I had proposed to her the year before on the banks of Lake Chocorua in New Hampshire under a full New England canopy of fall colors. I looked in her brown eyes that Sunday afternoon and *knew* that this was the very woman I wanted to spend the rest of my life with. I was overjoyed when she uttered that magic word, "yes." Then I got into my rent-a-car and drove back to New York. I had to wake up at 5:30 A.M. to go to work, after all.

For the first time since I arrived at Cramer & Company, I took a prolonged vacation, for my honeymoon. It was too late to cancel, and although a part of me wanted to sit in the office and take my beating like a man, I went to Antigua. During what should have been the happiest time of my life, I barely slept or ate at all. I sat on the beach, reading a few lines of a cheap novel, chain-smoking Cohibas, and counting the minutes. I was so totally preoccupied with what it would be like to walk back in and face Jim, I never relaxed, not even for a moment.

When I returned to the office, as the others attempted to fit in subtle and generic greetings, Jim stared stone-faced at his screens. He said nothing to me that day, and I did not catch him looking in my direction even once. It wasn't until the end of the week that he finally walked up to me and forced himself to shake my hand and congratulate me on my marriage. I could tell he didn't want to do it, but it was still a good sign.

I went back to trading and answering the phones. I started playing the syndicate game again. I was given the chance to help Jeff and Jim with *their* ideas. By the year's end, I had slowly but surely got myself off Jim's shit list. At least he was acknowledging my presence.

Yet, as I gradually clawed my way back into favor, something changed inside me. For so long, I had wanted only to prove myself in this world. With each achievement, I pushed the envelope further. I had *never* chased a goal like I pursued success at Cramer & Company. I worked my way up, but now I felt the ceiling begin to crumble. I could no longer summon the energy or desire to fight as I once did. I was finally, without question, "feeling the pain."

Chapter 15

SERIOUSLY UNDERPAID

ONLY ONE PERSON managed the impossible. In five years at Cramer & Company, I watched Jim find fault with everyone he came into contact with except Jeff Berkowitz. Jeff was director of research and knew how the game was played. More important, he had mastered the one essential thing: how to deal with Jim Cramer. Thanks to this ability, Jeff would eventually become a partner and have his name added to the door.

In saying that Jeff knew how to handle Jim I am in no way discounting his achievements. Quite the opposite is true. This talent was probably more challenging than Jeff's official job as director of research. Consider what happened to all the other stock pickers who ventured into our small world. Every year in January, a new analyst came to work at Cramer & Company. Every year, by March, the person had been fired.

The first analyst I worked with was Peter, a young guy who sold himself as a tech expert. He once had a nosebleed and walked around the office with two pieces of toilet paper sticking out of his nostrils. Jim and Jeff didn't like that much. Of course, falling asleep at his desk didn't help the cause. Before being hired, Peter indicated he understood software fairly well. Later we realized this meant he frequently played video games.

One of his picks was Panda Project, a computer manufacturer that made a PC with peripheral pieces that users could add or take out themselves. Panda, according to Peter, was "the wave of the future." The stock nose-dived into the low single digits as Cramer & Company continued to average down from the mid-twenties. Peter, like Panda Project, ended up a "mistake" Jim had to recover from.

The next mistake was Tim, a producer at the *Charlie Rose Show* on a night when Jim was a guest. Before taping, Tim told Jim what a big fan he was. In between compliments, he touched upon his own opinions on investing. Apparently, Tim had been reading up on one of his primary interests, Latin American markets.

The next week Tim became "director of foreign investments" at Cramer & Company. At first, Jim didn't talk to anyone else, but when Tim's portfolio drifted south with his markets, Jim wouldn't even say hello to the guy. We were all sick of hearing about the Colombian gross domestic product and the Peruvian consumer price index. Tim was gone a few months after starting.

The last outside help brought in was Greg, who stood about five feet tall and drove a brand-new souped-up black Porsche. A tech analyst at a pension fund, he had gotten to know Jeff at various conferences. Greg was certainly more legitimate than Peter or Tim, but that made no difference when he started losing money.

One of his biggest bets had been PictureTel, the video conferencing company. He knew the CEO pretty well and claimed this individual gave him "the insider's scoop." Greg was sure they were about to win a major contract. The big news ended up being the announcement of some new product even lamer than their original. After being the guest of honor at our Super Bowl party in January, he was fired by spring training. Mistake number three.

To understand the effects these individuals had on Cramer & Company returns, one need only see their P & L statements. Everyone who picked stocks, including me, was given an independent portfolio calculated separately from the firm's. This way Jim could assess exactly what one person contributed to or cost the firm. In 1996, for example, I could tell that I personally made over $10 million for the fund.

Being responsible for all the back office accounting, Clark and I were privy to everyone's P & L. Peter lost a couple hundred grand. Tim lost $1.5 million. Greg lost $2 million. Considering that the assets under our management were never less than $150 million, the most any of them cost the firm was slightly over 1 percent. To lose 1 percent was not even that bad a *day* at Cramer & Company. Still, Jim consistently blamed these people for much greater losses than they incurred.

Since a hedge fund is private, partners can't check returns in the paper, as the investors in a mutual fund can. So Marty and the other partners called Jim on a regular basis to check on performance. Given Jim's trading style, the fund was quite volatile, often having 5 to 10 percent swings. Each year at some point after Peter, Tim, or Greg left, there was an inevitable downturn. There was always a bad month, even in the best of years. These people were all, at one time or another, blamed for it.

Like Seth Tobias and Maria Bartiromo, these three young analysts found themselves on the Cramer & Company Ten Thousand Most Wanted list. How much Jim's resentment toward them grew with time was incredible. There was a company photograph taken right after Jim hired Tim. On Jim's request, Tim stood in the center next to our boss. Jim had a huge smile on his face and his arm around the guy.

"That fucking guy cost the firm so much fucking money, I want him *out* of the picture!" Jim declared not long after Tim's departure.

He meant literally.

No sooner did we get the retouched photo back than it had to be altered again. Now it was the ill-fated syndicate manager, Betsy, who had to be removed.

Of course, there was my own great rise and fall. I have no doubt that Jim also wanted me to leave. After I gave back a few million dollars, he made this clear. Because of my other roles within the firm and probably my relationship to Marty, I was able to remain an employee of Cramer & Company another few years. No one remained in Jim's good graces when it came to contributing stock picks.

At times it appeared that Jeff might be heading the way of the rest of us. When I first arrived, Jim and Karen had been invited to Ireland to visit a new Intel chip foundry. While they were overseas, something went wrong with a position. Jeff was in Jim's seat at the head of the desk, running the show, when Jim called. Jeff told him we had averaged down in a position that was now even lower, and Jim freaked. Jim wanted to know why he hadn't heard about this the previous time he called, which had been a few minutes earlier.

Keep in mind that Jim hardly *ever* left the office, and when he did, it would be incredibly nerve-racking for him. This is a guy who is used to sitting in front of his monitors from 5:00 in the morning until well after the close. Jeff was trying to get a word in, but Jim's voice echoed all the way from Ireland. He called Jeff a "fucking liar." Jeff had let him down in a *big* way.

This was the one time I saw Jeff reduced to tears. I don't think any of us in the office claimed to be especially macho, but we all knew that it wouldn't help our cause to break. Whenever Jim talked about ripping someone apart, he always mentioned whether the person "took it like a man" or not. He might still hate you with a passion, but at least you weren't a "fucking pussy," as he called one broker who begged forgiveness.

I was glad to see Jeff break for once. There were times when I locked myself in the bathroom until I could pull myself together enough to return for another round. All of us had been reduced to blabbering emotional idiots under Jim's constant verbal barrage. Yet, even though Jeff spent time in the doghouse, it was never as long or as severe as the rest of us experienced. Somehow, except for this rare occasion, he didn't seem to let Jim get under his skin.

Jeff seldom doubted himself. What appeared to be blatant narcissism was in fact an invaluable asset at Cramer & Company. Jeff never forgot that he had been a Goldman Sachs associate and attended Columbia Business School. He was smart and market savvy, and he knew it. Whereas the rest of us were all eventually degraded into accepting Jim's view of us, Jeff believed in himself. He always talked about his achievements, be it two dates in one weekend, his first summer bonus, or his new BMW. The same day he was called a "fucking liar" he told me on the way to the subway that his cleaning lady folded his underwear for him.

Jeff also refused to be given an independent P & L and insisted on "only contributing to the overall fund," as he termed it. Despite this self-proclaimed socialist ideology, Jeff said to me a few times, "I want to avoid being held a hundred percent liable for anything." The risk, he knew, was greater than the reward.

"Jim isn't going to give anybody too much credit," Jeff explained. "But he sure as hell might let someone have all the blame."

No matter what Jeff thought about a piece of information, he always presented it with room for adjustment. If Jim was negative on a stock, so was Jeff. If Jim was positive on a stock, so was Jeff. He recognized the parameters of his job and stayed within them. Jeff was the director of research. That didn't include deciding what to do with the information. Although he often thought he might be more in touch with these companies and know their technologies or events better than Jim, he always passed when it came to pulling the trigger.

Jeff wanted to have someone around to be impressed by his achievements. This was my role. I often listened to him carry on about the amount of money he made. Once Jeff took me along to Chase Bank to get a $1 million money order for a house he was buying in Westchester. After the teller handed him a check with a one and six zeros on it, he carried it in his hand down the street as if it were a subway token. We walked silently for a few blocks until we reached the corner of Wall and Water. He turned and looked me in the eye.

"You might think Michael Jackson making a hundred million dollars for *Thriller* was excessive," Jeff said, shaking the check in my face. "Then again, if there's a market for the music, let it play. Honestly, I'm *under*paid!"

"Of course you are." I smiled.

"Think about it," Jeff began to explain. "I am forced to deal with a madman on a personal and business basis day after day after day. The hardest part of my job is handling Jim Cramer. Jim does the important things right—he makes money. Otherwise, he's out of his mind.

"Just today we bought IBM on that stupid rumor . . ." Jeff continued as I followed him through the lobby of our building and onto the elevator. Jim had heard a rumor before the opening that an influential analyst was about to upgrade the stock and instructed Mark to buy a large slug. No sooner did we have our position than the market was selling off and we were down in the stock. Apparently, there had been nothing to the rumor. That's when Jim decided to take matters into his own hands.

"So Jim came into my office," Jeff explained, "and we started calling *every* brokerage house's IBM analyst. As usual, when we got them on the phone, Jim was doing all the talking. Morgan Stanley, Goldman Sachs, Merrill Lynch, Jim told them each that *they* should upgrade the stock. He was carrying on about how he just talked to Lou Gerstner, that things had improved remarkably in their core businesses . . ."

The elevator doors opened on our floor and I followed Jeff out into the hall.

"By the time we were talking to the last guy," he continued, "Jim just lost it. He started trying whatever he could. He told the guy that we paid his firm over $10 million last year, that his fat paycheck was essentially from us. He said that this was his chance to make a name for himself. Then he told the analyst he had no balls. He had no balls, and besides that, he might not have a future on Wall Street. 'I know people that can take care of a woman like you!' he screamed, then hung up the phone. Can you believe this shit?"

Jeff lowered his voice to a whisper as we walked through the gold-lettered front doors of our firm.

"Che-*ching!* Che-*ching!*" Jim was spinning around in his chair when we approached the trading desk. "Sell the last twenty IBM! Che-*ching!* Che-*ching!*"

"What happened?" Jeff asked.

"IBM just got upgraded," Mark explained, picking up a trading wire to give the responsible firm *another* big order.

"Nice work." Jeff gave Jim a smile.

Fool, I'm the kinda g that little homies wanna be like . . . Jim had hit the play button on his ghetto blaster and was screaming over Coolio in his high-pitched whine, adding lyrics to the old favorite:

Making money day and night, in the Wall Street spotlight . . . The imaginary gun was pointed toward Jeff and me, and Jim pulled the trigger. He blew smoke from the barrel before singing the chorus. *Been spending most our lives, living in a gangsta's paradise. Keep spending most our lives, living in a gangsta's paradise.*

"Like I said, I'm *seriously* underpaid," Jeff yelled into my ear. "If I tried to tell people what really went on here, I don't think anyone would even believe me."

Chapter 16

"I AM THESTREET. COM!"

DESPITE JIM'S "ORPHANS" INCIDENT and subsequent dislike of business journalists in general, nothing would discourage him from fervently embracing the spotlight. In addition to being a regular guest on CNBC, Jim appeared on *Good Morning America* and too many other television shows to mention. After his stint with *SmartMoney,* he wrote for *New York,* the *New York Observer,* even *Time.* It was usually when requested by popular demand to speak his mind that he could be witnessed in that rarest of forms. Having the chance to tell the world exactly what he thought put Jim in a *good* mood.

When *GQ* appointed Jim to be their financial columnist, an editor informed us that the magazine intended to throw him a private party at a trendy SoHo club, complete with "lots of models." The day of the big event, Jim and Jeff sat at the trading desk, flipping through the magazine, discussing which clothing brand names they liked and disliked. Jim wanted to be wearing only the most contemporary styles for the occasion. Kiel, his chauffeur, was summoned for a quick ride up to Barney's at Madison Avenue and Sixty-first Street *before* the market closed. They would make a few stops on the way, including one at Jim's "stylist." Jeff also insisted that they get "a quick manicure."

Clark and I arrived at the party that evening at 7:00, after rushing through our back office portfolio accounting. When we showed up at the club, Jim and Jeff were sitting alone at the bar, decked out in new Zegna suits with fresh haircuts and immaculate fingernails. The rest of the office arrived about the same time. We all pretty much hung out by ourselves for the first few hours.

Around 10:00, the fashionably late *GQ* crowd began traipsing in, and yes, there were some models. There was the clean-cut Wall Street crowd, complete with all our brokers showing their enthusiastic support, and then there was the skinny and funky designer crowd. Jim and Jeff had their pictures taken for the magazine with a blonde on either side and huge grins on their faces. When one of the models insisted that she recognized Jim, he was thrilled.

"I *am* pretty famous."

"I know I've seen you on television," she said, passing on a hors d'oeuvre plate as Jim grabbed two.

"Like I said, I get this *all* the time. People stopping me on the street—"

"I remember!" the blonde exclaimed.

"—asking me advice," Jim went on.

"You're a professional golfer!"

Jim nearly choked on his caviar, and Jeff quickly handed him a glass of Cristal to wash it down.

Jim's quest for recognition continued despite this setback. It wasn't long after that evening when he and Marty decided to start TheStreet.Com. Both were caught up with the potential of the Internet as a new medium to bring journalism to the people. The idea certainly was novel at the time. This was even before most Internet companies went public. The tide had yet to rise, let alone wash up. It would be the perfect business for a tied-in money manager like Jim and an experienced editor like Marty.

TheStreet.Com was to be a financial website with articles on the stock market written primarily by headliner Jim Cramer. A staff of business journalists covering various sectors and topics would also be hired, but Jim wanted to produce more than any of the full-time employees, sometimes writing two articles a day. With loyal fans paying to hear his beliefs on a regular basis, Jim was eager to commit himself even more to getting his opinions out to the masses.

When they decided to be business partners in TheStreet.Com, Marty Peretz and Jim Cramer were very close friends. They had known each other for years. Marty was the best man at Jim's wedding, gave him his first million to invest, and had helped raise a lot more money for him. Seizing the opportunity, Jim made it more than worthwhile for Marty and his friends. By almost any measure, it was a mutually beneficial relationship.

Despite this long personal history, Marty and Jim's business experience was not from an equal, hands-on basis. They were both savvy and accomplished but also independent and strong minded. Yes, the two spoke about everything on a regular basis, as I knew from overhearing too many conversations, but until now they had not tested their relationship with the unique challenges of a joint venture.

Jim always bent over backward for the partners, Marty especially. He would switch from swearing and throwing computers to answer their calls and ask them about their children's health and even discuss the weather if they wanted to. But as the years went on, and Jim's personal wealth and reputation grew, he became less of a sycophant. Jim was happy to take millions of dollars from investors, but to have to "*constantly* deal with them," as he began to say to those of us closest to him, "is incredibly tiring."

There had also been other evidence that maybe this friendship wasn't as sincere as Marty believed. The extent to which Jim resented Marty's asking him to hire me proved telling. Clark confided that Jim absolutely did *not* want to give me a job before our meeting and said, "I'm not going to be Marty's whipping boy." It wouldn't be until TheStreet.Com began to turn problematic that Marty began to see signs that Jim was less than genuine.

The differences between the two men developed on a trivial enough level. Jim was always busy and there was never a good time to reach him. Still, Marty usually called every morning around 8:00, one of our busiest times. When any of us told Jim that Marty was on the phone, he would roll his eyes, make some comment about Marty's timing, and then pick up the line with an enthusiastic greeting. No sooner would he hang up than he'd vent his frustrations.

"Marty thinks he can call whenever the fuck he wants," he announced to everyone in the office. "He expects me to put everything on hold for him."

With this backdrop, Marty and Jim's online magazine business took shape, grew, and managed to attract additional investment. The first five or six people were hired and started working in the back of Cramer & Company's offices at 100 Wall Street. Even though both Marty and Jim put a lot of time into the project, Jim felt an unquenchable need to constantly deal with some issue or another regarding TheStreet.Com. This was the same way he ran his hedge fund. He had to always be frantically busy doing something.

Although this constant effort was Jim's choice, he soon resented doing more work than Marty. By the time the company was only a few months old, Jim frequently complained, "I have to do everything." After TheStreet.Com offices moved to Rector Street, he insisted on going over there nearly every afternoon when the market closed to meet with the staff. As he saw it, he needed to be a hands-on manager. Marty, on the other hand, came once a week from Cambridge. Jim felt he was being forced to "do two full-time jobs."

Money also became a contentious issue. Jim wanted to throw more money at the project, while Marty held back. Jim was definitely aggressive with regard to financing the fledgling company. Marty, on the other hand, took a more conservative approach. He needed to understand where, why, and how the money would be spent.

"He's fucking cheap," Jim complained to us. "Marty wants something for nothing, just like the rest of the rich spoiled people."

What had been a somewhat understandable, minor disagreement was now getting out of hand.

None of this was easy for me to take. Marty had always been something of a father figure to me. To hear Jim criticize him initially made me cringe. I felt as if in some way I had betrayed Marty by condoning this behavior. Soon enough, however, just as I had accepted everything else, I accepted this. It was just another thing that I would have to live with to survive at Cramer & Company.

When dealing directly with Marty, Jim had kept his cool. Over the years when I'd see Marty, he would ask me how things were going. I always said "great." I never mentioned that he threatened someone's children and went to beat the shit out of a broker and threw a pencil at the secretary because she asked him what he wanted for lunch at the wrong time. It just seemed easier to say "great." There was a certain unspoken code between Jim and me—never involve Marty.

Marty had no idea how nasty Jim could actually get. When I first considered taking the job at Cramer & Company, Marty described Jim as a bit "intense," but stressed that overall he was "truly brilliant." Marty asked both of his kids, Bo and Jesse, to tell me what they thought of Jim, since they had met him on more than a few occasions.

Bo and Jesse were not quite as enthusiastic.

"Kind of crazy," they said, almost in unison.

Marty laughed and assured me that Jim wasn't, in fact, "kind of crazy." He refused to believe anything negative about Jim until TheStreet.Com situation grew out of control. Thus when it became apparent that the two men actually had differences, the conflict was already beyond resolution.

Jim quickly decided to let it all out now and resorted to the tactics he employed at Cramer & Company—he set out to kick some ass. When he thought things weren't going right, which was all the time, he screamed and yelled and threatened people's jobs. This technique worked in the financial arena, where he paid brokers and individuals millions of dollars, but at the magazine he only caused dissension. Much of the staff at TheStreet.Com could hardly put up with Jim. Many complained to Marty, who was surprised at Jim's behavior and unsure how to deal with it.

Finally there was an incident in which Jim wrote a string of scathing e-mails about Marty to someone at TheStreet.Com. In them he recounted everything I had already heard him spew about how much more work he was doing and the extra money he committed. He then went so far as to assert that Marty had no idea what he was doing. Inevitably, Jim had a falling-out with this confidant. Armed with loads of printed e-mails from Jim, the guy went to Marty. Jim and Marty stopped talking to each other, except in their weekly business meetings.

During all this I tried as hard as I could to disappear behind my screens on the trading desk. Whatever was going down, it got nastier every minute. By the time it came to a head in the fall of 1998, Marty pulled all his money out of the fund and urged many of his friends to do the same. A few partners, whom I knew personally through Marty, called me and asked, "Is Jim losing his mind?" I could only say that I'd lost mine some time ago, and perhaps I wasn't the best person to do a psychiatric evaluation on anyone else.

As luck would have it, that period was also to be one of the worst the international and U.S. markets had seen for some time. There was the Long Term Capital debacle and the global meltdown. Cramer & Company was getting pummeled. The partners who didn't jump ship with Marty began to question Jim's priorities. Everyone knew he was committing much time and effort to TheStreet.Com, and they apparently were concerned that he might be overextending himself. While you're making money in the hedge fund business, no one asks questions. In this case, Jim fielded calls from worried investors who wouldn't talk to anyone but him.

Jim and Marty's private feud became public knowledge, and their problems were documented in more than a few magazines. A friend of my father's tried to get me to speak about it to *Forbes*. The *Wall Street Journal* called me at home. There were a few negative articles on Jim, all of which he was sure Marty had planted.

"It's *disgusting* that someone would use their influence for such a low, self-serving purpose!" said Jim.

Sitting behind his monitors, obsessively watching every trade on the tape, he seldom got up from his seat. You could see in his eyes that he was going through a personal torture as intense as anything he had faced before.

If there's one thing that can be said about Jim, it's that *nothing* will keep him down. He would go on television as long they invited him, would keep writing for magazines that asked, and cer-tainly wasn't going to let up with TheStreet.Com.

"TheStreet.Com would be *nothing* without me!" Jim declared. "I *am* TheStreet.Com!"

As for me, each morning when I walked through the doors, I was met with contempt.

My sin? I was associated with Marty.

And as for the other partners who wanted their money back?

"Give it to the ungrateful *fucks*," our general proclaimed from his post.

Cramer & Company would survive without them.

Chapter 17

ANTI-DEPRESSANTS AND TRANQUILIZERS

"NICKY, YOU'LL BE RICH," Marty announced with an assuring pat on the back after our first discussion about Cramer & Company in December 1993. Besides understanding that I would gain incredible experience, I entertained certain fantasies. *Wall Street,* I kept thinking to myself. Maybe I *will* be rich.

In January 1996, after I finished my second year at the fund, Jim sat me down for another bonus meeting. After explaining that I was "a valued member of the team," he gave me a $100,000 bonus and raised my base to $50,000. Two years out of college, with only a bachelor's degree in comparative literature, I'd brought home as much as both of my parents combined.

By any measure, my material life continued to improve. A one-bedroom apartment on Eightieth Street just off Fifth Avenue replaced the studio on Thirty-ninth. Instead of fire trucks and protesting Cubans, I now had a tree to look at. I'd wake up on Saturday morning, stroll past the Metropolitan Museum of Art, and go for a run around the Central Park Reservoir. Afterward, I might have breakfast at E.A.T. on Madison Avenue, complete with a $5 glass of OJ and $8 potato pancakes. I had most definitely arrived.

My inner satisfaction, though, did not grow with my bank account. In my first year, making a much smaller bonus had thrilled me. Now, I was a Wall Street veteran. I'd read in the *Journal* of the seven figures others were getting. The money *always* could have been more. Cramer & Company just wrapped up a 60 percent year. Jim personally made over $20 million after taking his performance fee.

It was that January when Jim, still reveling in the wake of such a phenomenal year, threw a party for all of Wall Street. The idea was to say thank you to the brokers who covered us, which was certainly a change from ripping their heads off. During the year, these guys were the opposition. Feeling the rush of an eight-figure check in his account, Jim now saw everyone as his friend.

We hosted an all-expenses-paid trip to Atlantic City for close to five hundred people. We invited all our brokers, their husbands or wives, their assistants, even the people who helped us with our back office work. We rented buses that picked everyone up at points all over Manhattan, served lunch and beer, and showed the movie *Wall Street.* Jim insisted on *Wall Street* because he claimed that the character played by Charlie Sheen had been based upon his life.

"*Not* the going to jail part," Jim was quick to point out. "The scene where Charlie Sheen brought flowers into the secretary so he could meet Michael Douglas. That was *my* move to land a big client while starting out as a broker at Goldman Sachs. These fucking screenwriters, stealing yet *another* piece of *my* life to put up on the big screen!"

Once in Atlantic City, everyone checked into rooms in the Showboat Casino, where Cramer & Company T-shirts, baseball caps, and other merchandise awaited them. If you were really lucky, you could win a suede jacket with the Cramer & Company logo emblazoned on the front. There were certificates for free massages, manicures, and even a few strings of bowling.

After gambling, we all went to a huge banquet with massive $ sign ice sculptures that stuck out of a raw bar offering more shrimp, oysters, clams, and caviar than five thousand people could have finished. As if that weren't enough, for dinner we feasted on prime rib, Peking duck, rack of lamb, lobster, and all types of other cuisine, each prepared by a separate chef in a different corner. A twelve-piece band played. At everyone's seat were more Cramer & Company goodies. Umbrellas, squeeze balls, even mouse pads with Jim's very own visage. The only things missing: Jim Cramer masks that we all should have put over our faces.

The event climaxed with The Man himself giving a speech about how successful he had been, as indicated by the previous year's superior return. He thanked his dad, who was there, Karen,

Jeff, and finally the rest of us. Then, with tears in his eyes, he told every broker there that none of it would have been possible without *them.*

As I sat there at a table in the center of this huge ballroom, smiling and applauding with everyone else, I found myself wishing I were back in my room. As soon as the dancing began, I headed for the back door. By the time Jim had been lifted overhead by his adoring brokers, I was in bed. I learned of the highlights from Jim the next morning in yet another speech.

The following year, after another impressive return, Jim did it all again: gambling in Atlantic City, enough food for an army, more Cramer & Company souvenirs. Except the audience was filled with new brokers, most of the previous ones having been fired.

One Monday morning at the beginning of 1997, I walked through the door as usual, a little after 6:00, and found Jim laying into a Bloomberg customer service rep. The rep was as good as "shit-canned," Jim screamed. His service had been down for ten minutes. He handed the phone to me and said "deal with it."

As I listened to a young woman who had been reduced to tears explain that she could do no more, I attempted to call forth the blind aggression that was a requirement of my job. Jim paced behind his monitors, out of his mind because there were no scrolling headlines to read on his Bloomberg. His hair already jutted out in wild spikes. His lips moved as he mumbled something over and over again, which I couldn't make out. I thanked the woman and asked her if she would please keep me apprised. No sooner had the words left my mouth than Jim shot me a look of pained disbelief.

"Whose fucking side are you on?"

All I knew then was that I felt spent. Physically and emotionally exhausted. Each and every day was an ordeal at Cramer & Company. From January right through to the end of December, Jim's constant war only intensified with each successive year. I often dreamed that as he put more money away and added year after year of impressive returns to his resume, Jim would let up and finally enjoy the wealth and success he had achieved. That *never* happened while I was there. He grew only more intense. The bonus meeting became the *only* time over the course of an entire year that Jim said anything remotely positive.

There was by this time "Cramer, Berkowitz," and a wholly separate "& Company." A "them and us" doctrine now issued from the same general who once engendered team spirit and inspired our allegiance. The things that kept me going above all else—my desire to learn about Wall Street and to succeed in this world—were long gone. Mark gave up trying to be amusing. Clark knew to just keep his head down and mouth shut. Sal even pulled his tongue from Jim's ass. We were *all* tired.

The *only* thing left for me to focus on was the money. After my third full year at the fund, I made close to a quarter million dollars. Everyone I leaked the figure to was amazed. I knew I made as much as, if not more than, Wharton and Harvard MBAs at Goldman Sachs or Morgan Stanley. Still, here I was, at the start of a new year, and the money didn't make me feel any better. The one thing I looked forward to all year, the only recognition I would ever receive, was now over. It was day one of a new year. What did I have to look forward to?

I had long since figured out how it worked at Cramer & Company. Listening to that customer service rep crying, I knew perfectly well that it was either her or me. If the Bloomberg suddenly came up and running, I should take all the credit. As long as the service was down, I should pass the blame as fast and furiously as possible. I'm not sure what clicked inside myself that morning to reverse what took years to master. I elected to now be the target. I was losing it.

Barely a week later, several things went wrong at once. A single mistake by any one of us could send Jim over the edge. This time, we all contributed. Mark overpaid by an eighth of a dollar for a five-thousand-share lot of Intel. Sal failed to accurately calculate a new average on a thousand IBM calls. Clark let a trading wire ring *four* times. I neglected to put the firm in for an IPO that opened up a half a point. Jim stood up from behind his monitors and grabbed at his wisps of hair. His face was beet red and sweat shone on his forehead. He threw us all that trademark glare—a clenched jaw and menacing stare.

"You've all been incredibly overpaid," he announced, and turned and went into Jeff's office.

When I came out of my last bonus meeting in January 1998, one in which the figure grew yet again, the overwhelming feeling was no longer merely disappointment. The bonus didn't matter. I felt only utter despair. As I walked home across Park Avenue, toward Central Park and my Upper East Side apartment, past my $5,000-a-year health club, which I never had the energy to go to, I thought that my world was pretty black.

I soon engaged in a long discussion about these feelings with our office manager, Patricia. She listened patiently before putting a pen to paper. She drew a little diagram of the human brain and labeled different parts. She doodled something moving around inside the brain that she called "serotonin." The serotonin then came out of the brain and traveled in every possible direction. A "serotonin reuptake inhibitor," she went on while outlining the brain again, "keeps that stuff inside." Which I guess was supposed to be a good thing, because she'd been taking these inhibitors for some time, and yes, she did feel remarkably better.

We all knew Jim was supposed to be taking this medication, as he held his conversations with his shrink at the trading desk. Everyone could hear it all. We all also knew how much easier he was to deal with when he took this medication, which was *not* most of the time. In addition to the office manager, I learned, there were other people in the office taking antidepressants.

By the end of the week, I had gone to see a psychiatrist and spent two hours purging. I'm not sure if I paused for a breath the entire time, and the doctor just sat there and listened. I felt like absolute shit, and I had felt like shit for as long as I could remember. Then I wrote him a check for $500, and he wrote me prescriptions for three different kinds of antidepressants and an oversized bottle of Valium. Soon enough I was swapping tranquilizers with my co-workers.

Chapter 18

ZYCLON B

TOWARDS THE END of my time at Cramer & Company, Jim learned that we had become the subject of an SEC inquiry. All hell broke loose. He was the angriest I'd seen him since the time we were investigated after the "orphans" article. *No* one could be trusted and *everyone* was potentially responsible. Once again the enemy was trying to do us in.

The trade in question was the purchase of a large quantity of put options. "Puts" are stock options, just like "calls," that enable a player to make a leveraged bet when they think something is going to happen in a particular stock in a specific period of time. You use calls if you think a stock is going higher; you use puts if you think a stock is going lower. They give you the "right to sell" the stock at a given price. If the stock falls below that price within the given time period, the buyer makes money.

Our timing on this occasion may have been *too* perfect. The options we bought grew immensely valuable when the stock's price dropped. It always takes two to trade, and on the other side of this transaction was someone who had sold us the puts but now owed *far* more than he had initially made. It was most likely this seller who filed a complaint with the SEC, alleging an insider trading violation.

Puts and calls can be used to make a large bet with a minimum of committed capital. Because of this, options are the favorite vehicle for small investors who somehow have inside information. They sink their entire savings account into what otherwise would be a ridiculously risky speculation. Recognizing this, the SEC sits back and waits for the burned trader, like the one who sold us these puts, to complain. They inevitably do when staring at a massive loss. The SEC then traces this options purchase back to the original customer. Whoever was ultimately behind the complaint, they must have suspected we knew something that hadn't been disclosed to all.

"Yes, Karen, I'll bring home some *fucking* chicken!" said Jim on one occasion when the phone rang. While yelling into the receiver he scanned each of our faces, knowing that since this SEC investigation was all he cared about, it had to be all we cared about. Karen always gave Jim basic chores to do, and it annoyed him to no end. "I have a fucking *hundred million dollars* and Karen makes me *scrub the mother fucking toilet!*"

Weeks later Jim finally was informed that the SEC was not going to pursue the investigation further. He hung up the phone and threw his arms into the air in jubilation. We all knew the news before he even told us. Everyone could see in his face that once again Armageddon had been avoided. Jim did a victory lap around the trading desk, with all of us high-fiving our triumphant leader and Jeff waiting at the finish line. The two embraced.

"What a bunch of *jokers!*" Jim proclaimed about the SEC. We all laughed and applauded.

"My world," Jim declared proudly.

Standing on the sidelines watching all this, I realized there was no arguing with Jim Cramer. This was *his* world. Jim was the master of this universe. With this recognition, something in me gave out. I couldn't participate in the celebration. Inside, while smiling and cheering with everyone else, I had actually been hoping for a *different* outcome.

Then it hit me. This was Jim Cramer's world, but no longer mine. I had become the enemy.

Not long afterwards the fund was slowly bleeding to death. These were the days of "relentless shelling," as Jim put it. At the end of the first half of 1998, the fund had been up 9 percent while the major indexes rose more. Then in July, as the markets moved sideways, we gave up 4 percent, cutting our return to 5 percent. With each passing day of August, as the city baked in a late summer heat wave, the daily P & L continued its rapid descent. That month alone, Cramer & Company lost 21 percent. It was by far the worst period Jim Cramer ever had trading. The annual return showed a loss of 16 percent. In all his time in the business, Jim never posted a single losing year, let alone a double-digit one. Now Jim was out of his mind, and everything was falling apart.

Some people slow down when they're losing money. The idea is that obviously you're not making the right decisions if you're getting hammered. I've spoken with endless traders who all say that when things go south, you should step back and regroup. Start again small, most pundits advise. Once you get a rhythm and winning streak going, trading will be easy again. If you push it when your head's not on straight, you only compound the problem.

Jim thought the complete opposite. When things went badly, he fought like a cat. He tried and tried again until it worked, and would eventually reestablish his confidence. At least that's how it had gone in the past. This time Jim was trading like a bat out of hell, and finding that lone winner was as elusive as hitting the Lotto.

By this time Marty had pulled all his money from the fund. Other partners were constantly calling to express their worry and to ask when *they* could pull their money. Jim knew his whole career was crumbling before his eyes. He was beyond reason. Jeff barely approached him. The rest of us knew to speak only when spoken to.

More than a few times Jim spent the night on the back couch. He'd have on the same clothes from the day before and stubble shaded his face. The bags under his eyes made him look like he'd been beaten up. He took a few bites of food and drank cup after cup of coffee. All the while, he traded more than I ever witnessed. Clark and I were in the office until 9:00 each night, silently inputting all the prices.

As the cooler days of September approached, the losses slowed, but there was still no positive turn in sight. One Friday we came in facing a P & L that showed the firm down 20 percent for the year. To see a *red* twenty hit Jim like a bag of bricks. He had already been out of his mind, but it was getting worse. Every single position we put on went against us. We were getting slaughtered. He screamed trade after trade across the desk at Mark and intermittently turned and did the same to me. I was sitting next to him, trading options, since Sal had taken the day off. With twenty orders working, I was still placing more.

Trading options the way Jim Cramer traded options was not easy. With equities, Jim might say, "Buy ten thousand IBM" or "Sell ten thousand WDC." When these types of orders are coming at you nonstop, it's hard. But try five option orders at once. Buy 250 IBM March 85 calls at a half. Sell 500 WDC April 50 puts at two and three-quarters. You're not only dealing with a symbol and a quantity, but having to recall a strike price and expiration month.

That day, I had buys and sells of numerous quantities and prices working with many different brokers. I took reports of what was done and without a pause gave further instructions. Between orders, Jim was screaming something about "Zyclon B."

"Zyclon B! Zyclon B! Zyclon B!" he yelled, his eyes popping from his head. I thought for a moment that Zyclon B might be a stock, but Jim wasn't giving a number with it. Weeks later I learned that

Zyclon B was the poison the Nazis used to gas the Jews during World War II. I'm not sure why he kept screaming this. Maybe Jim, a practicing Jew, saw that day as his own Holocaust.

"Jim." I tried to get his attention. "Was that five hundred or a thousand Intel Christmas forty puts?"

As soon as I asked Jim to repeat a quantity, it was over. For a split second, he turned and looked at me as if I had been pumping the gas. He lifted the Bloomberg monitor next to him over his head and threw it at me. I barely had time to jump back before the screen shattered into a thousand pieces at my feet.

"*Mother fucker! Mother fucker! Mother fucker!*" Jim screamed as he flailed his arms in the air. He was jumping up and down, banging his hands on the desk in front of him. He picked up another monitor and threw it into the middle of the trading desk. He turned to the spares behind him, swinging his arms and legs spastically with full force. There was the dull sound of parts breaking in sealed cardboard boxes as the stack toppled over. Everyone around the desk stood up and stared at Jim. He lunged toward me, his hands balled up in fists. He glared at me with complete hatred.

"I am a fucking player!" he screamed, his eyes locked on mine. "I talk to Lou *fucking* Gerstner!!! I have made a mother fucking fortune for these people!!! I am a mother fucking player!!!" Jim's eyes were as wide as they could be, and he looked as if he would jump out of his skin.

"I talk to Lou fucking Gerstner!!! I am a mother fucking player!!!" Jim was leaning over his monitors, his hands reaching toward me as if he wanted to grab my neck and strangle me.

"I know, Jim," I said, backing away a few more steps.

"*I AM A FUCKING PLAYER!!!*"

"We can make it back!" Mark tried to calm Jim down. "We can make it back!"

Mark knew the root of the crisis. This was the worst stretch Cramer & Company had ever experienced. We were facing the unthinkable, a year so terrible it could easily have spelled death for a hedge fund.

Jim placed his hands on his hips and sucked in a deep breath. The room went silent, and smoke rose from the center of the desk where the last monitor had been thrown. Jeff stood silently. Clark didn't say a word, either. Mark wiped the sweat from his brow. Jim turned toward me.

"Get your fucking ugly face off this desk."

I turned, walked down the hall, and went out the front door.

Epilogue

FROM 1987 UNTIL 2000, the entire time that James Cramer was at the helm of his hedge fund, he averaged more than a 31 percent return per year. Even after he took his management fees and sizable performance bonuses, that figure came to 24 percent a year to the investor. During that period, the S&P and the Dow respectively gained 14 percent and 15 percent. There's no debating that he was one of the most successful money managers on Wall Street. Jim recognized the incestuous and manipulative nature of today's stock market, and used that knowledge for all it was worth.

As I consider what motivated Jim, I am reminded of the slow Friday afternoons when he got rolling on his stories. I heard all about his days as a reporter and his big break being the first to arrive at a Florida sorority house where Ted Bundy brutally murdered several women. I learned how he lived in Los Angeles, broke and homeless, sleeping in an old car with a gun next to him. He spoke about how during law school, he would sneak out of classes to check on stocks. And he spent endless hours talking about his early days in the hedge fund business, when he and Karen traded through thick and thin.

Once in a while, Jim revealed more intimate memories. Sitting at the trading desk twelve hours a day, he chose to be an open book. We understood what upset him, what made him happy, and what from his past affected him the most.

One of the most influential aspects of Jim's upbringing was his parents' economic status. He grew up in Philadelphia, the only son of a small business owner. Whenever Jim spoke of his childhood, he described it as lacking. Others always had more; he always had less. It was obviously significant to Jim that his family wasn't "upper" class. He wanted to even the scales like only someone with a chip on his shoulder could.

This manifested itself when as an undergraduate he campaigned to become president of the *Crimson*, the Harvard newspaper. He apparently had a contentious runoff with an opponent who was everything he felt he wasn't, namely, an elite snob born with a silver spoon in his mouth. That Jim emerged the victor was one of his greatest achievements. He had challenged the aristocracy and proved himself an equal. I'm not sure why the theme of needing to prove himself continually came up in Jim's stories, but it did. I suppose that may have been why he was always so driven, even after achieving incredible milestones.

In the end, Jim wanted only to be a star. Whereas once he craved financial success, upon finding it he needed something greater. The money and power weren't enough. It was his appearances on CNBC or *Good Morning America* that had Jim as high as I ever saw. Hearing from his fans often meant more to him than hearing from those closest to him. It was obvious that Jim sought, most of all, a larger spotlight. At the end of 2000, Jim walked away from Wall Street to pursue precisely this goal.

Whatever his motivation, he fought as no one I've ever known. There's no doubt he was absolutely ruthless in his pursuits, but that was just Jim's style. Anyone who dealt with him had to accept this. Most people would never liken a rough trading day to mass genocide. Then again, most people aren't cut out to outperform the market for more than a decade running. There was nothing Jim Cramer took more seriously than this business.

"We are at war. We are in a foxhole. *Everyone* out *there* is the *enemy!*"

With the stock market, there is only one absolute answer at the end of the day. In 2000, Jim's last year at the head of the Cramer & Company trading desk, he pulled off a 38 percent return. In a period when the Nasdaq posted its worst performance in history and most firms and individuals would have been happy just to escape with a modest loss, Jim Cramer had his best year *ever* in terms of outperformance. Such a finale is nothing less than astonishing. At the root of it all had to be a cunning genius and an unmatched commitment.

Each year at Cramer & Company, our Christmas party was held at a different restaurant. The first one was at Palio's, in the Equitable building. The last one was at Morton's, downtown. We'd always get a private room. We even once booked the whole restaurant ourselves. There was the usual Secret Santa and always a $500 gift certificate to Barney's.

Secret Santa was supposed to be lighthearted. We each picked a name out of a hat and tried to give this co-worker something funny. During my last December at the fund, we were going around the table, opening our presents. Finally we got to Jim. Sal had drawn Jim's name, and he bought him golf balls printed with the face of a Morgan Stanley options broker who had ventured several ideas that lost us money.

"This way," Sal explained to Jim, "you can knock the fucking guy five hundred yards for all the shit he put us in last year."

After he opened the gift, Jim was dying of laughter. His eyes were closed and his head turned the familiar bright red. He pounded on the table in front of him with his hands, cracking up to the point where I thought he might piss his pants. As office etiquette dictated, we all laughed, too.

"It's not that funny," said Karen, sitting next to Jim.

No one seemed to hear her.

"Jim, it's not that funny!" she said again, this time staring right at her husband.

All Jim could do was calm down for a minute, hold up a ball in one hand, point at it with the other, and crack up all over again.

"I *said,* it's not *that* funny!" Karen insisted. "It's not funny *at all!*"

"Why not?" Jim looked straight at his wife, and the rest of us began to gather ourselves.

"He's not that bad of a guy," she replied. Karen, of course, knew most of the people who covered our account, or at least the ones who hadn't been fired since she left to have Emma. "He was once your friend. A close friend, even." I'm not sure what came over Karen during her few years out of the trading fray, but she went on to say, "You know, Jim, you let business get in the way of friendship."

"Of *course* I do!" was all Jim could say.

For almost an hour, Karen and Jim screamed at each other out in the hall. When they reemerged, we continued the Secret Santa where we left off. Later that evening, Jim made a public attempt to appease Karen and change his errant ways. He stood up and raised his glass to make a New Year's resolution.

"I have something very important to say, and I want everyone to listen up! This will be the year," Jim said, "that I will make no enemies!"

None of us said anything for a moment.

Jeff smirked first.

"Maybe we should put a cap on the number," Jeff suggested, emboldened by more than a few drinks, "rather than expect absolutely no enemies."

"None!" Jim repeated. "And to prove it, I will pay everyone in this room a thousand bucks if I fail."

Two days after the party, a repairman was in our office, trying to fix the copier during market hours. The man started banging away on the machine, and the noise immediately pissed Jim off. He tried to ignore it, but that lasted less than a minute. He rose from his seat and went over to the technician.

"I'm sorry," Jim said. "Are we bothering you?"

"No," the guy replied.

"You're sure? You're sure *we're* not bothering *you* at all?" Jim clenched his fists and stepped right in the guy's face.

"No," the man repeated while stepping back from the copier to put more room between himself and Jim.

"Because I wouldn't want to bother you." Jim yanked a paper tray out of the copier and began slamming it on the top until it shattered, sending pieces of plastic flying across the room. "I wouldn't want *our* trying to manage *half* a *billion* dollars to get in the way of your *fixing a stupid fucking copier machine!*"

None of us ever asked for our money.

Jim Cramer put it out there every day—nothing was more important than making money. This was his commitment and it was destined to be mine as well. I learned the game he taught and was willing to go to any length to win it. I emulated Jim Cramer. I idolized Jim Cramer. I went to war for Jim Cramer.

Somewhere down Wall Street, I lost that fervor. As 1998 began, I found myself as confused as ever in my life, with little understanding of what was happening to me. The years of creating rationalizations for staying in such an environment had taken their toll. Anxiety attacks hit me every morning while I walked into work. My breath slipped away as I feared something not quite tangible. Sleep came only with sleeping pills, and I never felt fully awake. None of it mattered anymore.

One day I realized that this was a commitment I no longer wanted to make. At the time, my decision may have seemed impulsive. To turn and walk out in the middle of a vicious trading day was not how I planned to leave. But my number had been called from that first day I woke up before my alarm went off. I believe I stayed exactly as long as possible.

Of the other traders who were at Cramer & Company when I arrived that winter day in 1994, none are there now. Mark was finally forced out. For some reason, he never tried to pass the blame. I'm sure this led to his downfall. Sal is gone too. His years of being Jim's self-appointed mouthpiece didn't save him, after all. The last to leave was Clark, or Larry, as the rest of the world knew him. He obviously discovered that keeping his head down had ceased to work. Jeff is the only one still sitting at the Cramer, Berkowitz & Company trading desk, a whole new team surrounding him.

Even now that I've told my story, there is still a part of me that feels as if I failed. The old nagging doubts that I was somehow weak when I should have been strong. That somehow I let Marty down. I even sometimes wonder if I let Jim down. *Jim,* after all, would *never* have walked out, as I did.

Then I recall my last year at the fund. I would obsess and worry about catching a taxi *days* in advance. I locked my front door each morning, only to convince myself otherwise by the time I reached the subway. One day I went back three times. My right eye developed a twitch that seemed to kick up every morning right around the opening of the stock market. Obviously, the medication and the psychiatrist were doing nothing for me.

An evening came when I found myself at home before a computer screen, staring at the same old stock market data. I produced a new, blank page, and started to write. What flew out of me was a story about a young man who went to Wall Street with all the dreams and ambitions of any novice. In the hedge fund where he worked was a partner bent on doing whatever it took to maintain an edge, someone who would go so far as to commit murder to beat the market. He was willing to do *anything* to succeed.

For months, I went back to my apartment every night and worked on this novel. Since sleep was scarce anyway, I would write until 2:00 or 3:00 A.M. At the time, I didn't understand what it was that drove me to create this story. I only knew that doing it somehow helped me feel better. Now, years later, the value of finding solace in such an effort has grown clear. Once more through the practice of telling, I hope to find some peace.

Today I understand that a lot of people are reading this book because of James Cramer, but it was written to leave him behind. I'm off the tranquilizers, and feel a hell of a lot better. Some of the guilt is gone and a few of the battle scars have faded. I recently hung out an entire afternoon with my mother—during market hours, even. Beth and I have a daughter now, and there's nowhere better to be than at the playground with my family. I'm looking for a new job, but I'm in no rush to find one.